The
Clueless
Groom's
GUIDE

The Clueless Groom's GUIDE

More than Any Man Should Ever
Know About Getting Married

Peter van Dijk

Illustrations by Taylor Lee

New York   Chicago   San Francisco   Lisbon   London   Madrid   Mexico City
Milan   New Delhi   San Juan   Seoul   Singapore   Sydney   Toronto

The *McGraw·Hill* Companies

Library of Congress Cataloging-in-Publication Data

Dijk, Peter van.
    The clueless groom's guide : far more than any man should rightly know
about getting married / Peter van Dijk.
            p.   cm.
        ISBN 0-07-141372-3
        1. Weddings—Planning.   2. Weddings—Planning—Humor.
    3. Wedding etiquette.   4. Bridegrooms—Life skills guides.   I. Title.

    HQ745.D55   2003
    395.2'2—dc21   2002042881

8 9 10 11 12 13 14 15 16 17 18 19 20 21 22 23   FGR/FGR   0 9 8 7

ISBN-13: 978-0-07-141372-5
ISBN-10:   0-07-141372-3

Cover and interior illustrations by Taylor Lee

McGraw-Hill books are available at special quantity discounts to use as premiums and
sales promotions, or for use in corporate training programs. For more information,
please write to the Director of Special Sales, Professional Publishing, McGraw-Hill, Two
Penn Plaza, New York, NY 10121-2298. Or contact your local bookstore.

This book is printed on acid-free paper.

For Suki, with all my heart.

Contents

Introduction

How does this happen? You have a good job, great friends, a loving family. Life is good. Sort of.

Then you meet this woman. You meet this incredible woman. You think she's hot. She thinks you're cool. You don't know why yet, but this time it's different. You start making plans that stretch beyond next Saturday night. She leaves a toothbrush at your place. You don't mind. You remember her birthday. She remembers your birthday, your zodiac sign, your first dog's name, where your grandparents went on their honeymoon, and the anniversaries of your first, second, and third dates. Especially your third date.

While you remain utterly oblivious, you are inspected and accepted by her extensive and tightly organized cabal of friends and associates. Your friends, stooges that they are, somehow understand that they have to speak differently about this one. You meet her parents. She meets yours. Maybe she starts dropping some hints. Maybe she doesn't have to. But either way, both of you know where this is going. That thing that was different . . . this time it feels like family.

So, here you are. One day you're a regular guy with regular interests leading a regular life. The next day you're deeply mired in a morass of social complexity and political intrigue for which you are sadly ill equipped.

Congratulations on your engagement.

You are about to enter a new dimension. A dimension of china patterns, color schemes, and cummerbunds. You will hear things coming out of your mouth that will shock and terrify you. You will argue for a cut crystal pattern with the same general intensity that you now reserve for such important matters of state as whether Pete Rose belongs in the Hall. You will have an opinion about buffet versus sit-down, band versus DJ, and—God forbid—even daisies versus roses.

You will have arguments. Accept it now, you and your intended will have more than a few arguments. Most will be petty, some may be heated, but none should be long-lived. The vast majority of these arguments can be averted if you remember this simple fact: committing yourself to a lifetime of love, devotion, and fidelity is all about you and your fiancée. The wedding itself is not.

Your wedding is about you in the same way that the NBA All-Star game is about the basketball. You are a prop—a necessary one, perhaps, but a prop nonetheless. More specifically, you are a big, walking, talking, anatomically correct Ken doll. And believe me when I tell you that there's a reason why Ken never came with the kung-fu grip. You may have opinions. You may, and actually should, express them when called upon to do so. You must, however, back off when the real convictions come out, because, Ken, you are going to lose.

You are going to lose because she has been planning this day since you were still convinced you would grow up to be a fireman who plays shortstop in the bigs. You are going to lose because she has powerful allies, one of whom is likely to be your mother. You are going to lose because you still don't really understand for whose benefit this wedding is really being held.

There are those who would tell you that a wedding is the bride's day. They lie. Sure, she's the star of the show. She may even retain the illusion of control. But when push comes to shove, your wedding is most likely being held for the benefit of your future mother-in-law's cattiest friends and relatives. Depending on how many daughters she has, your new "mumsie" only has so many shots at showing her buds how a proper affair should be held. She will not be happy if this opportunity is denied. This is not to say that your wife, your future mother-in-law, and the ladies in her bowling league get to call all the shots. It's just that you would be well advised to approach all areas of conflict in a spirit of compromise.

As a final note before we get into the blow-by-blow, let's dispel one myth here. Your wedding will not be the most important day of your life. It probably won't even make the top five. The day you were born, the day you met your fiancée, the day she said yes, and particularly the birthdays of any present and future children all rank way higher. Your wedding is a celebration. So chill out, keep a smile on your face, and enjoy the ride. Believe it or not, very little of this process hurts, and most of it can be a lot of fun.

I would also tell you that it's all worth it in the end, but you already know that. You knew it the instant you recognized that this one was different.

CHAPTER 1

The Proposal

As in comedy, curveball hitting, and life in general, a proposal of marriage is all about timing . . . and blood-alcohol levels. When you do it and how sober you are at the time are far more important than the words, the setting, or the heavy equipment you've rented for the occasion. You only get so many shots at this, so you want to be pretty sure you are striking while the iron is hot.

So how do you know the time is right? Chances are that someone will just tell you. Chances are even better that that someone will be your current girlfriend. She may say it indirectly. She may say it straight out. She may even couch it in a terrorist threat. One way or another, she will tell you when it's time to pony up. Once she does, the clock is running, my friend, like Carl Lewis on a triple-strength dose of Benzedrine. If you don't pop the question before the buzzer sounds, you will only be left with two options:

1. Lose the girl.
2. Suffer the ignoble humiliation of succumbing to a flat-out demand.

Either way, you have lost the element of surprise, permanently surrendering the upper hand in this relationship. It's either over or severely crippled, because no one wants to start out a life of marital commitment because his girlfriend made him do it.

On the other hand, there are dire consequences to proposing too early. Public humiliation is a very real possibility. As are Hamletesque heartbreak and/or a near-fatal haymaker to the self-esteem. More important, you stand the risk of ruining a perfectly fun relationship by getting "all serious" too soon. Believe me, no self-respecting gent wants to go there. Can you imagine James Bond getting down on one knee and flashing the ice only to have the girl say, "I don't know, James. Let me think about it for a while."

I think not.

The answer we're going to be looking for here is, "Yes." Preferably, "Yes. Yes. Yes, baby. Yes, baby. Oh, yes. Yes. Yes."

So the key to this is (have you been paying attention?) *timing.* The trick is slipping the question in comfortably after she really, really wants you to—yet well before she is ready to slap you with the dreaded ultimatum. Depending on the patience, disposition, and relative pregnancy of your girlfriend, this window of opportunity lasts somewhere between thirty seconds and six months. Pay attention now, because these signals may just save your opinion of yourself.

Here's how to know it's time to pop the question:

- You catch her writing her first name followed by your last name.
- Under the gauze-thin cover of discussing a friend's wedding, she describes in excruciatingly painful detail what she would have done had it been hers.
- Her friends tell you. (Not that you asked them or anything.)
- Her "pappy" strongly encourages you to propose while showing you the barrel-end of the Remington 12-gauge he inherited from his father-in-law.
- She gave you this book, even though you aren't engaged.

How to know it's not yet time to pop the question:

- You catch her writing her first name followed by some other guy's last name.
- She says she wants to see other men, and you figure getting married would be a great way to stop her.
- You're in a bar, on your ninth round. And you met her after your fifth.
- After an evening of careful consideration, you decide she'd make the finest wife of all the lovelies in the overseas bride catalog.
- You bought this book for yourself, and she derisively asked you what you could possibly need it for.

Get the Story Straight

Now that you falsely assume you have the timing down right, it's time to decide how you are going to pull this thing off. Before you go rent the blimp and hire the mariachi band, pause and ask yourself, "Can I afford a blimp?" and, "Will I look other than ridiculous in a large, tasseled sombrero?"

Basically, what you have to figure out is how you want this event to feel. Do you want a big, gushing, over-the top gesture or a more intimate, romantic moment? Do you want this to happen just between the two of you, or would you like a sold-out crowd at Soldier Field to share in the festivities? There's no right answer here. Mostly just lots and lots of wrong ones.

One thing you should weigh into the mix is the indisputable fact that the manner in which you proposed will be chronicled and repeated at least fourteen thousand times over the course of your engagement. And another couple million times after that. Everyone will ask your fiancée how you proposed (at least everyone without that manly Y chromosome that keeps us guys focused on important issues like nuclear proliferation, garden pest control, and the shortcomings of the prevent defense). Your fiancée/wife/widow is going to answer these inquiries in fantastic detail. She will hold nothing back. Not one single, friggin' thing will she ever hold back. In fact, she will repeat every painfully awkward word you strung together, including every "ahh," "uh," and "ummm." If you were only marginally lame in your delivery, she will characterize it as "romantic." If you really got thick-tongued, it will be "cute."

She'll remember not just where you were when you proposed but everything about it. If you propose in a restaurant, she'll remember what both of you ordered, what color the napkins were, what the salt and pepper shakers looked like. She will remember Bob-who-will-be-your-server. She will remember what music was playing, what you were wearing, what scent she had on, what pocket you had the ring in, whether your voice cracked when you spit out the question, the precise nap of the jewelry box felt, the temperature of the room, and the dew point of the first post-"yes" kiss. Everything, everything, everything, everything. And just in case you missed the point, she will relay all of this everything to everyone she ever met or will meet until long after you are in the grave and she is throwing your pension, one quarter at a time, into slot machines at the Copa.

In other words, you may want to reconsider that cute little plan to dress yourself up like Cupid, encrust a little toy bow and arrow with red glitter, and loudly proclaim, "Thou hast pierced my heart. Marry me, my beloved." On the other hand, you sure as hell don't want to keep your lard ass parked in the La-Z-Boy and yell out, "Yo babe, wanna get hitched?" while she does the dishes. As a general rule of thumb, you're looking to avoid stories that are either too interesting or too dull.

Just Desserts

No matter what style of proposal you're going for, you want to have a plan. Of course, a certain amount of fumbling spontaneity can add to the occasion, but trust me, that will be there anyway. The key here is that the plan supports the mood you are trying to create.

If you want the experience to be an intimate moment just between the two of you, find a place you can be alone, light some candles, and open a nice bottle of wine. Not a bad start, particularly if the glasses are clean. Now slip some music on the stereo, maybe a little Barry White or Herb Alpert and the Tijuana Brass or something. If you already have an "our song," go 'head and spin it. (If your song happens to be anything by Herb Alpert and the Tijuana Brass, all the better. Scary, but better.) Don't smell bad, and wear clean underwear in case you get hit by a bus (or a bust, for that matter). Getting the picture here? Think through the details now. If this is your crib, rent a vacuum and clean the place up first. If it's her place, bring flowers. The whole idea is to create the right setting for the story.

Let's say you like the intimate thing, but want to heighten the drama a bit. How about driving to a scenic overlook, heading down to the beach, or out on the ferry? The Grand Canyon, Big Sur, the Empire State Building observation deck, or whatever the local equivalent is in your area will also work. The idea is to choose a place with grand scale that still allows you to find a little corner that feels semiprivate. By the way, these sorts of settings create some of the best stories in girlville because they sound just like the proposals they read about in soft-core romance novels. You know, "As the sun set crimson red behind the towering peaks of Capistrano, Raul looked deep into my azure eyes, and ripped off his shirt to reveal the smooth mass of his oiled chest. He manfully pleaded, 'Marry me, my love, and enchant me for all eternity.'" As a side note, those romance novels never say, "Having just picked up the spare in the beer frame, Bob looked deep into my azure eyes, ripped the seam of his pants to reveal U of O boxers, and said, 'So, you want to get married or something?'"

Another popular variation of the semipublic proposal is to pop the question at the local slop house. If you're going the restaurant route, make sure you set things up ahead of time. Letting the maître d' in on the plan should at least get you a decent table and a free after-dinner drink. He or she can also arrange more flamboyant gestures, such as having the waiter serve the ring in a covered dish. (Note that the assumption here is you have chosen a restaurant with a maître d'. Any restaurant that has a backlit menu hanging behind a counter is not likely to be deemed appropriate by your intended. "Go ahead, baby, supersize anything you like," just somehow doesn't have that certain romantic something, now does it?

If you do go the restaurant route and want to get a bit playful, be really careful where you hide the ring. It's not that you can't have some fun with this, just be selective about location. Appropriate choices include in a glass of champagne (make sure she doesn't swallow it), in a fortune cookie, or revealed with a flourish on a plate by itself. Bad choices would include being mushed into a pile of mashed potatoes, under a heavily caramelized desert, or anyplace she is not likely to find it.

Cue the Blimp

If you are the kind of guy who really likes to put on a show, you certainly have plenty of possibilities for popping the question on a grand scale. (Perhaps we should say "exploding" the question.) Pretty much every major league stadium and arena has a JumboTron that can be pressed into service for proposals. These all work a bit differently, so call the main number at the stadium and let the operator put you in touch with the right person. Make sure you include both of your names in the message, so that every guy who has a girlfriend with the same name as yours doesn't get in trouble. Try something like, "Marry me, Linda. I love you, Mike." Don't try something like, "Marry me, Linda. I love you and hate the Yankees, Mike." Remember you're playing to one fan here. Also, make sure you find out when your proposal is going to play so you can make sure your girlfriend is paying attention at the time.

While the stadium JumboTron is likely to be free, some of the other more outlandish media selections are going to set you back a bit. Skywriters, highway billboards, and the Times Square Jumbo-Tron will each cost you more than a few grand. Taking out an ad in the local paper runs anywhere from a few bucks for a classified to thousands for a full page, depending an awful lot on how big your local paper is. The nice part about some of these choices is that you get to include a picture as well as words. Perhaps you can get a buddy to take a picture of you in a tux down on one knee presenting a ring. Make sure that this is a buddy who is not prone to blackmail.

One word of caution on proposing in big, public venues. It's really tough to get shot down in a little restaurant. It's a whole lot worse to take a bullet in front of sixty thousand screaming fans. Before you call the JumboTron guy, be really, really, really, really sure that she's going to say, "yes." (And please, save the, "Yes. Yes, baby. Yes, baby. Oh, yes." for later.)

Assume the Position

Regardless of where, when, and how you do it, proper proposals are always done on one knee. This indicates to your future wife that you are fully prepared for a life of begging and pleading and will therefore make a good husband. It also has trophy value. You know all those people who will ask your fiancée/wife/widow how you proposed? The first follow-up question each one will ask is whether you got down on one knee. A "yes" answer to that question is hard currency in womanworld.

You may also want to give some consideration to the actual words you use to propose. I heartily encourage you to keep it short, sweet, and simple. You can't go wrong with, "[Her name here], I love you. Will you marry me?" You can go wrong with a book-length poem carefully chronicling every aspect of your affection in iambic pentameter. In fact, let's just make this a little rule here. If your proposal is so long or complicated that you actually have to write it down, then it's too complicated for actual use. (Remember: if your little brother gets hold of it, he will have a stripper read it to you at your bachelor party.)

Finally, if you're like the rest of us, you're going to get a bit choked up when the moment comes. Go with that, big guy. Whatever it is you need to say to the woman with whom you hope to spend the rest of your life, here's a chance you will never have again. Make it big. Make it small. Just make it a moment to remember.

CHAPTER 2

The Ring

Above all else, you need to know one thing about engagement rings. They are expensive. They are, in fact, so painfully expensive that the average man will audibly gasp and visibly pale at the mere mention of their price. That is, after all, the entire point. If they were not so expensive, our loving fiancées would not be nearly so insistent upon receiving them as tokens of our undying affection.

It pays to keep in mind that, to your fiancée, you are not just giving a ring. You are giving a sign of your willingness to go deeply into debt to purchase an item in which you have absolutely no interest rather than buy something you have deeply coveted since childhood. She will think that's really cool.

So exactly how big a sacrifice are we talking about? At the bottom end, plan on giving up your designs on a thirty-two-inch, cable-ready Sony wide screen with PIP, three input jacks, and a universal remote. If you really want to impress, you'll have to indefinitely postpone your hopes for a Dodge Ram pickup with towing package, reinforced skid plates, and a premium sound system.

It should be noted that the diamond retailers association recommends that you spend two months' salary on an engagement ring. Of course, if the diamond retailers association could get away with it, they would recommend that you deplete your entire net worth and resort to selling blood plasma to pay for their wares.

At this point, any rational man begins to consider the possibility of the big hoax. Admit it, you're zapping the commercials on "Monday Night Football" when you trip across a limited-time offering of cubic zirconium rings on The Home Shopping Network. You start thinking, "Will she really be able to tell the difference?" It turns out that the answer to your question is an undeniable, "NO." Unless your beloved possesses a degree from an advanced gemological institute, she will never know. There is, however, a hitch. Immediately upon receipt of her "expensive" engagement ring, your fiancée will insist that it be insured. To get insurance you will need an appraisal of the ring's value, and, alas, jewelry appraisers can tell the difference. Fret not. It was a nice try, and I applaud your resourcefulness. You're exactly the kind of guy who made this country great.

Now that you've shed a tear for your lost wide-screen TV or pickup truck, it's time to head out into the wilderness to hunt down a ring. I sincerely recommend that you proceed with caution. You are in uncharted waters here, and the sharks that will soon be circling you are very hungry indeed. It is safe to assume that in any transaction with an experienced jewelry salesperson, you will lose. These people will seek out your precise threshold of pain and belly up to your credit limit like an interior lineman at a buffet table. Resign yourself to it. The best you can hope for at this point is damage control.

Any jewelry salesperson worth his or her salt will begin by educating you in the various factors determining a diamond's value. This is the setup. Rather than gasping in horror, you will soon be evaluating the various components that can actually make a tiny chip of stone seem to possess the same value as an average bass-fishing boat.

The factors you will be duped into considering are widely known as the "four Cs": clarity, color, cut, and carat. Each of these factors has within its power the ability to increase a diamond's value and decrease your overall sense of financial security.

Let's begin with cut and carat, as these are the two components that ordinary, right-minded men can readily understand. Cut is "diamondese" for shape. The vast majority of diamonds come in five basic shapes: oval, pear-shaped, marquise, emerald, and round (or brilliant-cut). More recently, novelties such as heart-shaped diamonds have also been made available. (If the news escaped you, take it as a sign of mental health.)

Of the five, oval, pear, and marquise have the ability to make a stone appear larger. Round-cut stones are generally the twinkliest. Emerald-cut stones are considered by many to be the most elegant. None of this matters. The only important consideration here is which cut your fiancée prefers. Believe me, she will have an opinion on this and, if you were listening, she will have made this opinion clear long before you set out shopping. For a clue, listen to those catty and/or admiring comments she makes about other women's rings. There is a message in those comments. It is directed at you and it is not unintentional.

The next factor you will be forced into considering is carat. Carats are the weight units with which gems are measured. They are very small units, indeed. In fact, it takes 142 of the little suckers just to make up an ounce. For those of you accustomed to making the argument that it's not the size that counts, you will quickly discover that your argument does not hold much weight in this realm. Size counts. A lot. Not coincidentally, it costs. A lot. If you are at any point tempted to sacrifice size to purchase a diamond of absolutely pristine quality, resist the temptation. On a routine basis, your fiancée will be asked how many carats her ring weighs. She will never be asked the more obscure quality ratings. She will want an impressive answer.

Clarity is measured by the amount of imperfections, known as *inclusions*, that mar the diamond. You can go pretty far along the rating scale before the difference is actually visible. Despite the almost certain protestations of your jeweler, I recommend you trust your uneducated eye in determining what is acceptable. Work down the scale from near perfect to total crap. When you start recognizing flaws, go back up a step or two to find your mark.

As for color, several tints are available in addition to the standard clear diamonds. Some of these are less expensive than the clear ones. Some are radically more expensive. Once again, it behooves you to determine if your fiancée's tastes run toward colored rather than clear diamonds.

You may have noticed that the focus of this chapter so far has been exclusively on diamond engagement rings. There do exist, however, women who prefer other gems. If your fiancée is among them, consider yourself fortunate. With some exceptionally rare exceptions, you will save at least a small wad of c-notes off the price of an equivalently sized diamond. If you have found a woman who actually prefers such sentimental tokens of your affections as a Cracker Jack ring or a cigar band, kneel down before her in devout worship. She has been sent to you by the gods.

The Setting

Now that you've depleted your entire net worth and gone "all girly" studying this cut-color-carat crap, you must be out of the woods, right? Not until you've thought long and hard about how you want that stone set, young man.

Your first call here is picking the type of metal used for the setting. You have three choices: yellow gold, white gold, and platinum.

Unless you know for a fact that your fiancée wants otherwise, choose platinum. It's far stronger than gold, and the lighter color will make her diamond more sparkly. It's also more expensive than gold, but at this point you might as well throw in the towel.

Regardless of which metal you choose, you will be presented with three basic ring designs: prong set, flush set, and bezel set. Generally, your safest bet is the classic prong set. It holds the diamond high off the band, making that puny little chip look like something relatively special. Prong settings also let more light hit the stone. This causes the diamond to sparkle and your fiancée to get all giddy. If you go this route, try to get a six-prong setting instead of the flimsier four-prong setting. The extra prongs hold the stone in far more securely. (And who doesn't like their stones held securely, eh?)

Flush-set rings embed the stone into the band. The upside to this setting is that it protects the stone from all manner of assaults. Think about this design if your beloved intended works construction or is otherwise active. You may also want to suss this one out before you pull the trigger. It's a less conventional choice.

Bezel-set diamond rings are a variation of the flush setting. This setting employs a full-metal collar, usually gold, that wraps around the diamond like an inebriated prom date. It's a sassy little modern look. Don't get it unless you really know she wants it bad.

Let the Fleecing Begin

So where should you go to hand over your life savings for an upscale pebble? This is going to depend an awful lot on where you live and who you know. First, understand that where you shop is going to make a huge difference in what you pay. There can be as much as a 100 percent difference in the price of a stone depending on where it is purchased. Second, understand that there are unscrupulous diamond dealers out there who will try to rip you off. If you are shopping at anything other than the most reputable national firms, it pays to check out any diamond merchant with the local Better Business Bureau.

That said, there are really four types of places to shop for diamond rings: chains, local jewelers, highbrow emporiums, and online sweatshops.

Department stores and mall chains are a relatively low-price alternative for guys who are on tight budgets or who are just plain cheap. Apparently, this includes almost all of us. Big retailers like Sears, JCPenney, and Zales peddle the great majority of the retail ice in this country. The upside to these joints is that you'll get a reasonably good deal on an OKish ring. The downside, no little girl dreams of the day when a man gets down on one knee and pulls out a box from Wal Mart.

If you're going to pop for more than a couple grand, you may be well advised to check out a few of the local jewelry stores in your area. Here's where you'll really want to rely on referrals from trusted friends and family, perhaps backed up by a report from the BBB. Not all of these guys are petty thieves, but apart from guys selling diamonds out of briefcases on the street corner, this is the realm where you're most likely to get ripped off. Depending on where you live, however, you're also likely to find a better selection of serious stones at the local jeweler than you are between the toasters and lawn mowers in aisle seven.

Really looking to score some points? Unless your local guy is in Palm Beach, Beverly Hills, or the like, you're going to be running with the big dogs like Tiffany, or the major mambo mastiffs like Cartier, Harry Winston, and Van Cleef & Arpels. Yes, the average schmuck can pick up a teeny-weenie little ring at Tiffany for a grand. That, however, is not what these places are made for. They are made for hurting guys who can afford to take a real beating. These guys have rings at prices that would make Bill Gates sweat. Forget giving up the pickup truck. Top out at Harry Winston and you're giving up designs on a fifty-foot Bertram offshore convertible with twin 600 bad-boy diesels.

Finally, online sources for diamonds are growing in number. At least they were until all those annoying little people decided the companies they invest in should actually make money. However, before jumping online whole hog, make sure your stone comes with a grading certificate from the Gemological Institute of America (GIA) or the American Gem Society (AGS). You should also make sure the site has a liberal return policy. You're not going to get a whole lot of help here, so you probably want to make sure you're pretty well educated on your four Cs before getting virtual with the cyber boys.

Shop Before You Pop

There was a time when an upright gent just wouldn't think about popping the question without a ring in his pocket. Those days are gone. Now, more and more couples head out together to shop for an engagement ring like it's the new family Buick.

The practical upside to this approach is first, even after reading this far, you don't know squat about diamond rings. She does. Second, there's also a pretty good chance that you don't really understand the style of ring she covets. There's a really good chance she does. In fact, there's a really good chance that her wishes are as precise as a sidewinder missile at point-blank range (and only marginally less destructive). Add to this the fact that she knows the local jewelry landscape, is willing to devote more research time, and is a better negotiator than you are, and you'd think that shopping for a ring together is the obvious route.

It isn't. Let's face it, getting engaged just ain't about what's practical. It's about what's romantic. And you found that one perfect woman who thinks that nothing in the world is more romantic than your sorry ass, down on one knee, pulling a little velvet box out of your pocket. When you really get down to it, that's what you need to know about diamond rings.

CHAPTER 3

A Future In-Law Primer

I t has often been said that when you marry your wife, you marry her whole family. While this is generally true, it only goes so far. For example, it doesn't mean that you will have "marital relations" with her whole family, unless you happen to hail from one of the more remote sections of the Appalachians. The extent to which you do become part of your wife's family, however, does have some alarming implications. For starters, you know all those people you have been sarcastically deriding for the past several years? You're one of them now.

Let that one sink in for a moment, Sonny Boy.

Ready to move on? Consider this: being one of them means that sooner or later, they are going to start treating you like one of them. That means no more, "Give Sissy's boyfriend the nice chair and fetch him a nice big piece of pie." It means, "Get your lazy ass off my chair and fetch me a big piece of pie."

If you want a fairly accurate barometer of how your relationship with the future in-laws will develop, take a good long look at how they interact with each other. If you like what you see, skip this chapter. You'll do just fine on your own. The other 99 percent of us will catch up with you in a few pages.

First Impressions

Depending on the length of your courtship and your proximity to her family, you may already have well-established relationships with your future in-laws. These relationships may begin to evolve in a somewhat unsettling manner, but at least you are working from a set base. We'll deal with you later.

The tough cases are you guys who are only getting to know your future in-laws during the stress of planning a wedding. It's even tougher if you are meeting them for the first time as their little girl's fiancé. You, my friend, are trying to pull off the quadruple toe loop on some very thin ice indeed.

If you've managed to avoid meeting your fiancée's family until you're already engaged, you probably live some distance away from the old homestead. This makes your neck of the woods a very desirable place to settle down, even if you are permanently stationed aboard a Polaris class nuclear submarine patrolling endlessly under the polar ice cap. Now that you've come ashore, Sailor Boy, let's see what we can do to keep you out of trouble.

The one thing you have to understand is that when you meet your future in-laws as a "serious" boyfriend or fiancé, you have virtually no margin for error. If you're some guy she's dating, they at least have the option of holding back judgment on your relative lack of personal hygiene and/or job prospects. Rather than going to all the trouble of getting out the shotgun and loading it with some quality birdshot, they may decide it's easier to see if you'll get better or just go away. On the other hand, when you come in as the selected candidate, you must be dealt with and you must be dealt with now. This being the case, assume that every word, every action, every everything you say, do, emit, or reveal can and will be used against you in the court of public opinion. Now, more than ever: think, think again, think once more, speak. Oh yeah, and remember to relax and have fun with these people. They're family.

You Stand Before the Court

Whenever you come into contact with your future in-laws, it pays to remember that you are being evaluated for your ability to take care of someone they love very deeply. If these people are at all human, they will want to see that you can make her happy. Unfortunately, the fact that you actually do make her happy is only sort of relevant. You still have to prove that you can make your future wife happy in the precise manner that her parents think she ought to be happy. This rarely, if ever, coincides with a little thing we in the business like to call "reality." Let's say your fiancée is a board-certified cardiologist with a trust fund that's larger than the Argentinean national debt. Your in-laws will still want to make sure you will be able to buy your wife a comfortable home in a town with excellent schools on that salary you're pulling down at the Jiffy Lube. And it wouldn't hurt if you could also swing a membership over at the golf club, too.

Of course, your breadwinning prospects are just the price of admission. You are also being judged on how well you tend to your fiancée's emotional needs. No problem, right? You two have tons of fun together; you worship the ground she walks on; and you truly, deeply care about her happiness. Again, this is barely relevant. What you have to do now is show your future in-laws how happy you can make your fiancée while she is being made venomously miserable by their mere presence. You're not going to get out of this with a box of bonbons and a five-dollar bouquet of daisies, are you now?

Chill out. You're not going to win this one, so you might as well relax. Just keep your cool and duck when the pots start flying. You are never going to step in and solve the arguments they've been having for decades. You really just want to avoid starting any new ones of your own.

Don't Just Sit There, Say Nothing

One thing you might want to consider is staying away from these three topics for . . . oh, let's say forever:

1. Religion
2. Politics
3. Sex (Get out the highlighter here and put a fat, yellow stripe across this one. The only sex you can really be talking about here is the steaming hot monkey love they assume you are having with their daughter.)

The more extreme your views on any of these topics, the more you want to avoid them in the early going. If you are a devil-worshipping communist who enjoys the occasional sheep-dip, you may even want to consider having your larynx removed. It can only get you in trouble.

Of course, religion, politics, and sex only occupy the first three slots on the universal list of topics you should avoid. To round out the other several hundred thousand items on the list, you'll have to test the waters for yourself. In some homes, for example, your cheery approval of artificial turf and the designated-hitter rule are roughly akin to a fondness for child molesting and grave desecration. Other conversations to avoid might include, but are not limited to, any that begin with the following phrases:

- "This sounds crazy, but . . . "
- "Let me tell you about my first wife . . . "
- "Here's what I learned from my years in San Quentin . . . "
- "Man, that's a heck of a goiter you got there, can I . . . "
- "Here's something you probably don't know about your daughter . . . "

In fact, it may be simpler to list the topics that you can talk about:

- The weather

Damage Control

Whether you met your fiancée's family last week, or you've known them since you moved in next door twenty years ago, let's assume you've had plenty of time to screw everything up already. You went ahead and did something crazy like totaling Dad's new Jag or talking about something other than that cold front that's moving in. Here's what you've got to do to make everything good again:

Eat shit. And I mean eat it like you have never eaten before. I'm not talking about some little thimble-full off of the dollar menu here. I'm talking about one heaping, Thanksgiving feast with all the trimmings. Start by apologizing fervently, vowing never, ever to repeat the offending transgression. Not sure what you did wrong? No problem. Apologize in some vague way that makes it sound like you actually know what you did. Something like, "I just feel awful about this whole situation. I'm truly and deeply sorry."

After the apology, try some sort of gesture of atonement. If it's her mom that's ticked off, try flowers. Take her dad to the ball game or a strip joint or something. (If you're in trouble because you already took her dad to a strip club, try getting her mom lots and lots of flowers.) The overriding point here is that damage control with the in-laws is all about being willing to make the effort. As in all family matters, the right and wrong of the issue is rarely important. The matter of who's willing to bend first to make the relationship work is always important. If the transgressions are all trivial, forget the fact that you are innately superior and they're morons. Life is better for you if you give a little.

Establishing the Boundaries

There is one particular area where you should never, ever give an inch. Your in-laws need to understand that they are not always welcome at your home. In fact, they need to understand that they are rarely welcome at your home and never welcome to just pop by. No matter how friendly it sounds or how helpful they intend it to be, "pop by" is just one step down the social acceptability ladder from "drive by."

The degree to which you will have to make the boundaries clear rises inversely with the distance from your house to your in-laws'. If they live in Peoria and you live in Tasmania, you can probably get away with a simple request to please call before hopping on a thirty-hour transpacific flight. If they live any closer, more drastic measures will be called for. If they live next door, nothing short of a crocodile-infested moat will suffice. If you happen to live in their house, find a good place to hide and don't come out until you can afford the overnight fees at the homeless shelter.

In an effort to keep the peace, you might start by promising them that you will never stop by their place without calling first. When they completely miss the point and give you an open invitation to come anytime you want, say something like, "I could never do that. I think that going to someone's house without calling is as rude as blowing your nose on someone's sleeve without asking." When this doesn't work, try a more direct approach. Something like, "Come to my house without calling and I will cut you." It should at least be good for a laugh.

Unfortunately, the only way you are likely to ever convince your in-laws that you and your wife need some privacy is to raise the specter of them walking in on you and their daughter making the beast with two backs. In fact, the first time they "pop by," you and your fiancée/wife should instantly get naked and start making out with great enthusiasm. If that doesn't cure them, go ahead and shoot them. There is no other alternative.

By the way, it should be noted that your family will now be someone's in-laws, too. The same rules that apply to her family have to apply to yours as well. You just don't have to like it as much.

Choose Sides

When your fiancée/wife has an argument with anyone in her family, she is always right and the other is always wrong. If this argument happens to be with her mother, then she is very right and her mother is very wrong. This is true no matter what the argument is about, largely because the merits of your fiancée's case are always the same. Agree with her and you can continue having sex with her. Agree with her family, particularly her mother, and you can't. Is that a compelling argument or what?

By the way, this logic should be equally compelling when your wife has an argument with your mother. Sure your mom endured agonizing pain to give you life. Sure, she worried and toiled and struggled to give you everything you needed and most of what you wanted. But that couch ain't getting softer, now is it? Do everything you can to keep the peace, at least at a surface level. But make sure your fiancée/wife at least believes that you are really on her side. Besides, it's a great chance to pay your mom back for not letting you get that dirt bike you wanted when you were twelve.

CHAPTER 4

Setting the Date

Now that you've bought the ring and bagged the girl, it's time to get down to business. The first stop on this freight train is setting a date for the deed. Before doing so, however, be cautioned that choosing a date is sort of like buckling into a roller coaster seat. Once this puppy gets rolling, you're not going to get much rest until the screaming stops.

Understandably, many couples prefer to bask in their engagedness for a while before they lock and load. Most of them quickly discover that this is more annoying than relaxing. In fact, the arguments for picking a date shortly after announcing your engagement are fairly compelling. First, having a set date allows you to put a timeline in place. That way you can enjoy the illusion of proceeding in an orderly manner. Second, by having a date, a clever young scholar like yourself will be able to discern which season it will be when you get married. This will help you two lovebirds decide everything from your color scheme (yeah, weddings have color schemes) to what the bridesmaids will wear (yes, you love it) to what you and your guests will pay for accommodations (either a lot or a very lot). These, however, are just some of the practical trivialities. The real reason you want to set a date early is so that you have a short answer to the first question everyone asks after you tell them you're engaged. (In certain cases, the first question may actually be, "You're kidding, right?" Even then, the next question is likely to be, "Have you set a date?")

Before you set a firm date, you should speak with all of the principal parties: parents, clergy, psychotherapists, astrologers, and those you intend to be in the bridal party. One good way to proceed is first to have some sense of when you want to get married, then approach your families, shamans, and other prospective members of your wedding party to find a weekend when everyone is available. You are likely to be talking about a date pretty far into the future, so specific-date conflicts are not highly likely. You are more likely to have conflicts that spread across an entire season. For example, if you know that your fiancée's parents always spend their winters in a nudist colony in Malta, you may want to think about something other than a January wedding. Likewise, if your brother isn't up for parole until next June, you might want to look past the spring.

Some Dates Are Better Than Others

Much like finding your intended in the first place, you'll quickly discover that some dates are better than others. First, let's look at some of the big boundaries. If you choose a date within three months of announcing your engagement, pretty much everyone will assume your fiancée is pregnant. If she actually is pregnant, this will work for you. If not, don't do it unless you just want to mess with your grandmother's head for a while.

On the other hand, any engagement of more than two years calls for extreme extenuating circumstances. Being in school tends to be the most popular, but there are any number of others. Of course, a long engagement precipitated by excessive youth begs the question: "If you're not grown-up enough to get married, is being engaged anything more than a fancy name for going steady?" You may think so, I don't. In my book (and let's face it, your name ain't on the cover) engagements of more than two years are justified only by either extended commitments to the more extreme branches of the armed forces or long jail sentences. If your engagement involved the exchange of goats between your parents in any way, shape, or form, a longer engagement might also be called for, particularly if your fiancée has yet to be born.

So let's assume that none of these apply. The first thing you and your intended may want to decide is which season would be best. This may or may not have something to do with where you intend to be wed. Think long and hard about holding your wedding in whatever qualifies as the off-season in your neck of the woods, particularly if you plan to hold any part of the ceremony outside. While it might be charming to hold your wedding during the blizzard of the century, it will create more than a few logistical hurdles. Also, keep in mind that virtually all tuxedos are ill suited to tropical climes. A backyard wedding should be illegal in Florida during any month when the children are out of school. If your location has anything called "mud season," "black fly season," or "tornado season," you may also want to get out that fat magic marker and cross those off the calendar.

Your not wanting to be way off-season doesn't mean that being right on-season is without peril. If you live in one of those places that has a well-defined season, you may want to work around that, too. Places like beach towns and ski resorts can be great places to hold a wedding. However, both you and your guests are going to pay double for pretty much everything at the peak of the season. You will also have to book all facilities and accommodations much farther in advance and may also have to provide firmer guarantees on the hotel rooms you are holding. If this works out, you'll still have to deal with all of the traffic and overcrowding these places generate at the height of the season. If you have your heart set on a wedding in a resort town, a good fallback might be the fringe season. You get better deals, smaller crowds, and more flexible vendors.

Of course, not all places have such seasonal extremes. Unfortunately, that doesn't mean you get a free pass. The most popular months for American weddings are August, June, and September, which are all nice months for weddings. Just understand that the wedding infrastructure will be more stressed during these months than it will during the rest of the year. If you can avoid peak season, you will have more choice of venues, bands, and the rest. You'll also be in a better negotiating position throughout the process.

Regardless of the season, most weddings are held on Friday, Saturday, or Sunday at 11 A.M., 2 P.M., or 4 P.M., so why should you be different? Yeah, you could get a great deal on a wedding hall if you held your wedding at 5 A.M. on a Tuesday morning, but even your mother wouldn't be able to make it.

Should Your Wedding Be a National Holiday?

You would think that all of your guests would appreciate you planning your wedding for a holiday weekend. They'll get a whole extra day to travel. They will have much more "companionship" on the roads. Booking their airline and hotel reservations will be a far more fun and exciting challenge. And, heck, who ever has plans for those annoying three-day weekends anyway?

You'd think they would appreciate it even more if you held your wedding around the Christmas/Hanukkah/New Year season. They're out shopping anyway, so what's it hurt to throw another present in the basket? Even better, they'll actually get a chance to go to a big party in December. An end-of-the-year party!!! Now that would be something special.

OK, OK. Usurping everyone's holiday weekend with your wedding is not necessarily obnoxious by definition. It does, however, raise the stakes tremendously. If you are going to deny your friends and family their traditional 4th of July softball game and pig roast, you better hold your wedding where they can at least catch some fireworks.

If you're going to hold your wedding on New Year's Eve, you better provide noisemakers, bubble machines, and lots of drunken revelry of the highest order. (If the drunken revelry can directly involve the bubble machines, so much the better.) In other words, if you are going to plan your wedding for a holiday, it's thoughtful to incorporate some of the traditions of that holiday and make them even more fun.

One caveat: Super Bowl Sunday is never a good day for a wedding, unless you are taking all of your guests to the game.

What's Taking So Long?

So you've picked a season, lined up the bridal party, and are all set to go. Now that the big calls have been made, you should be able to slap this thing together in a few months, right? I mean how long can it take to buy a dress, bake a cake, and invite a whole bunch of friends and relatives out for dinner and a trip around the dance floor?

The truth of the matter is that planning a wedding hardly takes any time at all . . . if the plan is to club the lass on the head and drag her by the hair back to your cave. If you wacky kids are considering something a bit more formal than that, this is going to take a whole lot longer than you could possibly imagine.

How much longer? The answer you're looking for here is somewhere between one and two years.

No, I'm not kidding.

Yes, that's years.

At this point it might be helpful to gain some perspective. Let's take a quick look at things that can be accomplished in about one year:

- ❖ The Empire State Building can be built.
- ❖ A three-month-old human being can be made from scratch.
- ❖ The Earth can complete a bajillion-mile orbit around the sun.
- ❖ A wedding can be planned.

Of these four, the only one that everyone will tell you is on a breakneck, God-I-don't-know-if-so-much-can-be-done-so-quickly schedule is . . . the wedding.

Go figure.

Depending on where you live and how insistent you are on particular venues, your wedding might even bust right through the two-year barrier. In fact, some of the most popular wedding locations in the biggest cities are consistently booked two years out—more for some of the most popular weekends.

So, let's say you somehow can't deal with the reality that you're going to be in wedding-planning mode longer than you were in grad school. You decide to be a bit more flexible on the wedding-hall front. In fact, you'll go ahead and hold your reception at the Waffle House if that will move the schedule ahead a basketball season or two. You are never going to guess what the next big holdup is.

Get this: *Bride's* magazine suggests that your bride choose and order her wedding gown at least eight months before she intends to wear it. In case you don't speak "Girl," the key word in that last sentence was *choose*. This, I promise you, will not be accomplished in one quick trip to the mall.

I wouldn't blame you if you're sitting there thinking, "This guy has to have it wrong. It can't possibly take longer to sew a dress than it takes to build a four-thousand-square-foot house, hike the entire Appalachian Trail, or complete an entire hockey season." Would it were so, *mi amigo*. Would it were so. At least the dress will have good company in wedding purgatory. The bridesmaids' dresses might also take months, your invitations will take weeks, and your wedding cake ain't exactly working on the Betty Crocker schedule. Grin and bear it, Buckaroo. At least you'll have some more time to save up money to pay for this thing.

CHAPTER 5

Setting the Budget

'll assume that you already know that this wedding thing is going to be expensive. Heck, you've thrown parties before, maybe a few really big ones. Back in your school days, you might have even held the purse strings on one of those over-the-top, frat-boy extravaganzas—the one with the tower of kegs, live bouli-bouli band, and seared meat barbecue for 625 of your very closest friends and classmates. A wedding couldn't cost more than all of that, could it?

We pause here to laugh.

OK, OK, that was a schoolboy thing, and you did steal most of the meat out of the cafeteria freezers. The wedding has to be more in the range of that swank Shriner's ball you threw down at the Clam Shanty. That fine-fezzed affair had sit-down prime rib for one hundred, a geezer swing band, door prizes, and the works. A nice wedding would probably fall in about that range, right?

Sit down, dear boy. This is not going to be easy.

If your fiancée has determined that you are going the full-blown, traditional wedding route, the budget for that magical night at delta delta delta may not even cover her dress. The Shriner's ball tab may make a solid dent in your reception bar bill, particularly if your harder-core friends are still serving time from that bachelor party incident. Then again, it may not even cover the champagne if you have a serious enough wine snob in the family.

The ugly truth is that this one party *di tutti* parties is going to cost you far more than all other parties you have ever thrown . . . combined. The even uglier truth is that you are about to be married to someone who passionately believes that blowing that kind of jack on cake, a veil, and toasting cups is money well spent.

It would not be considered unmanly to weep at this point.

So exactly how much is this going to cost you? In generally ascending order of importance, four questions will determine your wedding budget:

1. How many people will be attending?
2. How formal a wedding do you desire?
3. In what part of the world will it be held?
4. How much you got?

Head Counts Count

While it generally draws the most fire, the total number of people at your wedding is only the fourth most important cost factor. It is far cheaper to have five hundred people over to the house for a weenie roast than it is to fly ten of your closest relatives to the Right Bank for an intimate affair at the Georges V. That said, for any given wedding style and level of trim, the more people you have, the more your wedding will cost. This is because most reception expenses—from the bar bill to the cake—can be pegged to a head count. (For some ideas on how to keep the numbers down, check Chapter Seven, "The Guest List." Go ahead, we'll wait.) Small is indeed beautiful. If you are working with a really tight budget, however, small only gets you on the team. You have a lot of work to do before you're in the game.

Style Is Substantial

Next up on the "Wheel of Gonna Cost You a Fortune" is the relative formality of the affair. In fact, extreme choices in terms of style could easily catapult this cost factor to the head of the class. The ultimate swank-a-riffic, high-society wedding—such as one might witness on "Dynasty" reruns—can yield some pretty impressive numbers. On the other hand, a backyard barbecue following a simple ceremony under the old oak tree—such as one might witness on "Green Acres" reruns—should cost little more than your average 4th of July picnic. Overall, the continental divide has party-like gatherings on one side, and Weddings with a capital *W* on the other.

Generally speaking, anything tagged as "Wedding" carries a premium. (Any of you with a boat may already be familiar with this phenomenon. Screw, 1¢. Marine screw, $867,452.) The more shopping you do in the traditional wedding venues, the more likely you are to pay the premium. For example, a very elegant, well-tailored white dress can be had for one hundred dollars. A cheesy, off-the-rack wedding gown goes for almost a grand. A sheet cake down at Costco retails for twenty-five bucks. A wedding cake of comparable magnitude will set you back several hundred simoleons. Get the picture?

After all this, your beloved intended still has her sweet little heart set on re-creating the Charles and Di wedding. (Except for that part where you play hanky spanky with Camilla Parker Bowles while the Lord High Examiner inspects your bride to affirm her virginity.) So what's a guy to do? While you may not be able to divert the mighty juggernaut of her stylistic intention, a few key words sprinkled around at the right moments can have some mitigating effect. By all means, avoid words that connote cheapness, and employ words that imply romance. For example, suggest an "intimate" wedding instead of a "small" one. Speak of making your wedding "spontaneous" instead of "informal." Plea for the "elegant" rather than the "simple." This also works on the downside. You are not opposed to "formality"; you are against "stuffiness." Make sure you put on that really sincere, thoughtful face when you pull these bunnies out of the hat. You know, the face you use when trying to convince her that a Hummer really is safe and practical transportation.

Escape from Manhattan

Working our way down to the third most critical cost factor . . . weddings are kind of like Kmarts. The things that matter are location, location, and location. Think about it. The most lavish ball you can throw in rural Idaho is likely to cost an awful lot less than a relatively small gathering in midtown Manhattan. There's a lesson in this. If you are from Los Angeles and your fiancée is from French Lick, Indiana, you may be well advised to go check out the VFW down by Larry Bird's spread. In addition to adding some rural charm, you can pull off a really nice wedding in single-stoplight towns for pennies on your big-city dollar. This general strategy can be applied even if both of you are from high-rent districts. Pick a cool resort town, and hold your wedding there in the fringe season. Not only will all the big bills be smaller, but it will also help keep a lid on the number of guests. The ones who really want to be there will make the trip. The marginal guests won't. Both have to send crystal goblets. (Is this a great scam or what?)

That Big Sucking Sound

Finally, we get to the only cost factor that is really going to count: how much you and your families are willing and able to part with.

Wedding budgets tend to work kind of like military procurement contracts. The original figures serve only to mock the final tally. Unless you and your fiancée are really serious about keeping it simple, wedding expenses creep up and up and up and up. They usually stop somewhere around 10 percent above what all of you have. The caution here is to know the upper limit early in the process. That way you can wave to it as you go zooming by.

Bottom Up or Top Down

Now that you know some of the factors that will cause you pain, you may want to figure out the damage. There are two basic ways of doing this. As previously suggested, you can sit down with your families, check your bank balances, and determine a bottom-line budget for the wedding. Alternately, you can begin with the wedding of which your fiancée and her mother have always dreamed. Then count the number of guests who are likely to attend, and go get some numbers. Both of these routes will take you to the same place. Some of you will be pissed because the wedding will not be everything you always wanted it to be. Others will be pissed because it really is ridiculous to spend so much money anyway. As long as you're in the latter category, don't worry too much.

Of the two approaches, you are probably better off getting at least a general target number before diving into the nitty-gritty. It won't yield you any better results, but you may save a little time in the process. If you're working on a tight budget—let's say the cost of a brand-spanking-new Jeep—it's pointless to check out any place where the doormen dress like members of a marching band. If you have a fat wad—say the price of the average American split-level house—you may not have to pour over the menu at the Olive Garden. The other nice thing about this approach is that your fiancée will be partially spared the annoying experience of falling in love with things she can't have. (Sort of like how you feel about the Batmobile.) That will save both of you a lot of pain.

And the Bill Goes to . . .

The protocol dictating who pays for what parts of a wedding is as carefully proscribed and steeped in tradition as the changing of the guards at Buckingham Palace. It also doesn't mean jack squat. For example, your mom, the CFO, may not be entirely happy with the wedding your fiancée's dad, the supermarket bag boy, can afford. While no one has thrown away the old playbook, the rules have clearly changed. Perhaps the best approach is to start with the traditional guidelines and adjust heavily for relative wealth, expensiveness of tastes, and general sense of fair play. That said, here's what you and your family would traditionally pay for:

- The bride's wedding and engagement rings
- The marriage license
- The officiant's fee
- The bridal party's bouquets, corsages, and boutonnieres
- Gifts for ushers
- The rehearsal dinner
- The honeymoon

The common split among the traditionally minded is that you would pick up the rings, the usher's gifts, and the honeymoon, and your folks would pick up the flowers, the officiant, and the rehearsal dinner. Unless you throw really lavish rehearsal dinners, it is good to be the parents of the groom.

On the other hand, here's what your bride and her family would traditionally pay for:

- Everything else

Just in case you forgot, everything else includes, but is not limited to:

- Your ring
- Invitations, cards, and announcements
- Wedding gown and accessories

- Ceremony location
- Flowers for ceremony and reception
- Gifts for bridesmaids
- Photography
- Music for the ceremony and reception
- Limousines, gondolas, horse-drawn chariots, and so forth
- All reception costs: booze, food, hall rental fees, decorations, cake, coat check, valet parking (are you getting the picture yet?), champagne fountain, bride/groom cake toppers, going-away outfits, bail for the overtly drunk and disorderly, and so forth

The common split among the traditionally minded is that the bride may or may not pick up the bridesmaids' presents and your ring, while her parents pay for everything else. In other words, the traditional father of the bride gets hosed like the traditional pretty boy in a prison yard. Sure you can hold out for the traditional ways of doing things, but really it's a bit of a scam, now isn't it? I mean, you weren't so hot on tradition when it came to that premarital sex thing, now were you, Mr. Nineteenth Century? In all fairness, you should angle for a more even split along somewhat Marxist lines. Those with more pay more. Those with less pay less. No matter who pays, there must be plenty of vodka! Huzzah!

One Last Little Big Thing

Let's say you've haggled and scrimped and saved and trimmed and finally hammered out an acceptable solution at a price point that leaves you bloody but not beaten. Here comes the killer deathblow from hell: tips. By the end of your reception, you'll be looking at more upturned palms than the grand marshal of the International Slap-Me-Five Parade in Sheboygan, Wisconsin. The damage here can be catastrophic. Depending on the size and scope of your reception, tips could add a budget-busting couple of thousand smackers to the bottom line.

I know what you're thinking. Couldn't you just cut the tips, knowing that you're cutting out of the party early anyhow? Yup. Would that make you a maliciously stingy, malevolent little low-life weasel? Double yup.

Unless you're the sort who regularly stiffs Jenny-who-will-be-your-server down at the Sizzler, you pretty much have to add at least 15 percent to the top of the reception bill to lube all the palms requiring grease. Believe it or not, here's what the menagerie expects to be fed:

◆ Caterers usually build a 15 to 20 percent tip into their bill. If the caterer or reception-site manager has really been bending over backward for you, it is customary to throw him or her an extra buck or two per guest.

◆ If the caterer did not include a tip in the bill, the waiters have 15 to 20 percent coming.

◆ Barkeeps should get 15 to 20 percent of the bar tab if it's not included in the catering contract. If it is, the beerslinger still merits an extra 10 percent.

◆ Coat-check girls and valets get a buck or two per coat or car. Sure the coat-check girl simply puts a coat on a hanger while the valet sprints across a freezing parking lot. But, she's cuter, so she gets twice as much anyway.

◆ Limo drivers get a 15 to 20 percent tip. More if you got jiggy in back.

◆ Musicians and DJs get tipped about twenty-five clams apiece, if and only if they didn't play that "Bride Cuts the Cake" tune.

◆ Lacking adequate union representation, florists, bakers, photographers, officiants, and especially videographers are not tipped.

CHAPTER 6

Legal Matters

For many of us, getting married isn't quite the radical life-transforming event it was for generations past. No livestock is exchanged. You don't have to bequeath your kingdom to anyone. And let's be honest, your wedding night sure as heck ain't gonna be the first time you've seen her in her skivvies. In fact, if you already live together, being married will certainly make you feel different, but it probably won't radically change the way you live on a day-to-day basis.

In the eyes of the law, however, living together and being married have virtually nothing in common. Like the Yankees and

◆ *The Clueless Groom's Guide* ◆

the Red Sox, they carry with them an entirely different set of expectations and responsibilities. The big difference is that, as soon as you ink the deal, your relationship is not just between the two of you anymore. It's between the two of you and your local, state, and federal governments. As a result, being married will change your tax status, the price of your car insurance, your creditworthiness, and a host of other issues great and small. And if you thought breaking up was hard to do before, wait 'til you try it now.

On the Plus Side

Married couples enjoy quite a number of legal rights that are not bestowed upon lowly heathens cohabiting in sin. Although it is no longer a crime to share linens with a consenting member of the opposite sex, few states offer any real legal protections for unrepentant sinners.

So how does this come into play? As soon as you and your bride put your John Hancocks on the marriage license, she will become your legal next of kin. That means that she will be given right and responsibility to make decisions for you if you become incapacitated. Let's say you finally eat the cheese fry that breaks the camel's back. As they rush you to the hospital, she can sign the papers saying it's OK to surgically repair your sorry ass. Or, let's say that deep in your dotage you decide that public urination, playing bagpipes, and howling at the moon would all make fine hobbies. That signature on the papers authorizing your one-way ticket to the booby hatch will be hers.

Now let's say you are killed in a prison riot. If you and the better half are simply unwed fornicators, she has no legal claim to your earthly possessions, unless you have a will specifically claiming that she does. The deed to your house, your prized collection of roadside attraction shot glasses, your bass-fishing boat . . . none of it goes to her. All of it could go to that worthless, no-count brother of yours who couldn't be bothered to send you an occa-

40

sional carton of Marlboros when you were in the stir. If you are married, however, your wife automatically gets all your earthly possessions, even your tattered collection of nudie magazines.

In addition to the rights of survivorship and commitment to mental institutions, you'll enjoy other killer bennies of marriage. You may well have an easier time getting a mortgage, adopting a child, and buying insurance. You are also likely to pay less for life, medical, and auto insurance, as you are now more apt to a longer, healthier, and safer existence. Just don't let any of these people actually meet you before you ask for the discount. You might scare them.

Death and Taxes

If you need further proof that getting married will change your life forever, look at the dramatic impact it has on the two areas of life that no one can avoid: death and taxes. Let's start with the less painful of the two.

You're going to die. Sorry that I have to lay that on you at this time of great joy and celebration, but that's the fact, Jack. When you do, someone gets all that stuff you've spent a lifetime amassing. If you've been paying attention, you now know that the automatic first someone on that list will be your wife. If you've amassed enough stuff by the time you die, the automatic second someone on the list will be your Uncle Sam. Will this be a big problem for most of us? Absolutely not. We're talking millions of simoleons here before Washington takes a slice. But still, wealth has a way of creeping up on some of us. (Which is why most wealthy people are such creeps.) Now that you're a real grown-up with real responsibilities, you need a real grown-up will. At the very least, get one of those will-maker software packages to spell out your basic intents. If you get any kind of a career going, or expect to inherit any sort of serious assets, you should see your local shyster for a custom job. If either of you have kids from a previous marriage, you should definitely get a will. Just think, if Cinderella's dad had paid a few crowns for a proper will, she wouldn't have had all that unpleasantness, now would she?

As for the second inevitability, your entire tax picture will change now that you are getting married. Every year, when you submit that pack of lies you call a tax return, you will be asked if you are married. Unlike the situation at most airport cocktail lounges, you will not be able to lie about this. (Don't ask me how, they just know. Maybe they send the FBI out to check for the telltale dent in your ring finger or something.) The fact that you are married will in some way impact how much you pay in taxes. Despite efforts to reduce the marriage penalty, you are likely to pay higher taxes if both you and your wife earn money. If one of you lies around in your underwear all day eating potato chips and watching reruns of the "Beverly Hillbillies," your tax bill is likely to fall a tad. You should also know that your marital status only counts on December 31st of a given tax year. If you get married on New Year's Eve at 11:59 P.M., the feds will consider you married for that whole year. If you expect to get whacked by the marriage penalty, you may want to consider hemming and hawing until 12:01.

Prenuptial Bliss

Asking the woman with whom you plan to spend the rest of your life to sign papers giving up her rights in case you dump her like a bad habit can be, well, tricky. Those who know say that the best approach is to be straight, honest, and fair. Tell her that you love her, but that you want to make certain that all those you love are protected. Either that or get her all liquored up on expensive swill and tell her she's signing yet another model release for a *Girls Gone Wild* video. (Actually, all the fun-sponges down at the municipal court would say it doesn't count unless she knows what she's signing.) If you want the agreement to stick, she should have her own lawyer check everything out before signing.

Here's how you know that you need a prenup:

YOU	HER
Loaded	Stacked
Three kids	Younger than any of them
Business owner	Working girl
Landed aristocrat	Landed you

Perhaps a far more likely set of circumstances in your case would be:

HER	YOU
Gay divorcée	Gay
Country club member	Cabana boy
Wealthy heiress	Impoverished airhead
Jet set	Busboy

While the rich spouse–poor spouse situations get all the press, any number of down-to-earth situations actually might warrant a prenup. If one or both of you are involved in a business partnership, your partners probably should insist on it. If you were to be divorced, they might very well end up being partners with your ex-wife. Entertainment value aside, spending all future partner meetings discussing why you had to go diddle that cocktail waitress at the dog track could be somewhat counterproductive.

You might also want to think about a prenuptial agreement if one of you has lots of debts and the other has lots of assets. For example, let's say your fiancée has carefully saved up a fund to pay for her electrolysis while you've maxed out every credit card you could obtain during one long and painful evening at Caesars Palace. A good shyster should be able to set up something where your wife's assets are guarded from the wrath of your creditors. In fact, if either you or your wife has significant assets or debts, it might be worth a few bucks to see if there's a solid reason to have your union negotiated by attorneys.

Signing on the Dotted Line

Getting your marriage license is kind of like a particularly festive day at the DMV. You wait on line, interact with stone-faced government bureaucrats, sign a lot of papers, and pay a fee. Except this time around, it's fun, exciting, and kind of oddly adventurous.

Every state has its own wrinkle on the marriage thing, so it pays to call your local city clerk's office or town hall to find out what you will need to bring. You should do this about one month in advance of the ceremony so you will have time to get your papers together, get blood tests[1] back, and still make it to the church on time. Some states also have a waiting period between the application and receipt of a license, but it's usually not more than a week.

While you can expect some variation on the theme, here's what you will have to do to get your marriage license:

- ◆ You and your fiancée will have to show up together so the state can see that she actually wants to marry you no matter how poorly that reflects upon her judgment.
- ◆ You must both have some proof of who you are, how old you are, and what country you hail from (e.g., birth certificate or passport).
- ◆ You need proof of divorce or annulment from any training marriages.
- ◆ In some states, you need completed blood tests and doctor's certificates from both of your sawbones.
- ◆ In many states you will need to supply witnesses, like your best man and maid of honor, to verify that neither of you was henpecked into getting married.
- ◆ You need between ten and thirty dollars to pay the license fee.

---

1. Don't worry about the blood test thing. They're only checking for grotesque diseases that could kill you, cover your genitals with unsightly boils, or permanently deform your future children. No big whoop.

In addition to these, you will be required to make certain wiseacre cracks to showcase your boyishly charming sense of humor. These include:

- Make some comment about being "licensed to operate that thing."
- Playfully suggest that you go for either the moose-hunting or bass-fishing license instead of the marriage.
- Display some dramatic mock hesitation when asked for the ten-dollar fee, pretending to consider whether getting married is really worth that much money.

Are We There Yet?

No. Getting your license just means that your state has granted you permission to get married. To be a real, honest-to-God, legally binding union, your marriage license must be signed by a qualified religious or civil official and returned to the proper state office. At that point, and only at that point, has the fat lady hit the high note.

CHAPTER 7

The Guest List

Before you and your intended sit down to hammer out your guest list, you may want to take a few simple precautions. Unload and safely store away any firearms that may be on the premises. Remove any blunt objects and/or easily hurled items from the immediate vicinity. Put some soothing music on the stereo, dim the lights, and swallow a fistful of Prozac. If negotiators from the UN are available to mediate the peace talks, you may want to consider hiring them.

In other words, this guest list thing can get ugly. And we're not talking run-of-the-mill, everyday ugly. We're talking Ernest Borgnine with elephantiasis on a bad hair day.

Here are some of the ground rules: once upon a time, it was customary for the guest list to be divided equally among the bride's and groom's families, regardless of who was ponying up the cash for the event. This worked well until the Russians launched *Sputnik*, the Pill hit the market, and we all got the crazy notion that it might be better to get married at an age when you can legally buy Boone's Farm Apple Wine from the neighborhood liquor store. These days, with engaged couples being old enough to have play dates without their parents' permission, it is broadly accepted that you may have some friends of your own who you would like to invite.

A good place to start is to break the list into three parts. Your folks get a third. Her folks get a third. You and your fiancée get a third. If any of the 'rents are divorced, they split their third according to the division of assets clause in their divorce agreement (or 50/50 if you want to be all pedestrian about it). This may create a situation where your future father-in-law is footing the whole bill and getting only one sixth of the seats. That's what he gets for not producing enough virile X chromosomes.

Now you have your starting point, there are two ways to proceed. You could take a look at the budget, figure out how many guests you can afford, divide by three, and get to work. The good part about this approach is that you get to the most entertaining arguments faster as everyone quickly bumps up against a hard limit. An alternate approach is to have everybody make a list of all the people they would like to invite. Then tally up the numbers and see what you've got. If you are anywhere near striking distance, you may be able to serve cheaper food to more people and save yourself a lot of aggravation. The nice thing about this approach is that it puts people ahead of crab puffs. You start with who you want at your wedding, then figure out what you can afford to serve them.

Of course, more often than not, what you can afford to serve to that many people is a Dixie cup of Pabst Blue Ribbon and a small wedge of government surplus cheese. This, I'm guessing, will not pass muster with the future missus and her retinue. (And, let's face it, a sophisticated man of the world such as yourself will insist upon at least enough Pabst at his wedding to fill a proper beer funnel.) At this point, you're going to have to figure out some way to cull the herd. You can accomplish this any number of ways. None of them works to avoid all the ensuing arguments, but they will at least give you a somewhat objective framework. That way, when you start screaming at each other, you'll have a little bit more ammunition.

Before you get to the hard calls, you should figure out your core group of come-hell-or-high-water invitees. These should include you, your fiancée, really rich people who will definitely not be able to attend, and wealthy octogenarians with no heirs. If you have any stamps left over at this point, you should consider adding your parents, siblings, and grandparents to the list. Throw in your bridal party; your bosses; and a few mandatory cousins, aunts, and uncles, and your core group should be pretty well complete.

This is where the fun starts. After establishing your core group, let's say you could cut back on the marzipan bridal statuary and make room for another 50 people. You check the long list and discover that only 847 names are left on the list. This is progress. Now all you have to do is run them through a few screens, and you'll be within a marching band of your number in no time at all. Here goes.

Screen #1: Cut the Kids

This is one of the most common and least fun methods of getting the numbers down. The upside of this approach is that you quickly cut dozens of people in a socially acceptable manner, while greatly reducing the odds that someone will loudly announce his or her need to go potty while you are reciting your vows. The downside is that you will miss a lot of great photo ops, and the only people hanging spoons on their noses at the reception will be your ushers. (Not to mention the fact that your great-uncle Bob may still loudly announce the need to go potty while you are reciting your vows, and it will not be nearly as cute as when a four-year-old does it.) One note of caution: the no-kids screen should not be applied selectively. Parents get offended when you only invite other people's children. Establish a minimum age, sixteen or eighteen are popular cutoffs, and only make exceptions for members of the bridal party and your kids from previous marriages and/or NBA careers.

Screen #2: Cut the Colleagues

While it is generally considered sage career advice to invite your immediate supervisor to your wedding, that's about where the butt-kissing obligation stops. If you have an administrative assistant, particularly one who helped you out with some of the wedding work, it's also good form to invite him or her. This should be done if for no other reason than to prove to yourself that you are not just a pandering toady, you are a pandering toady with a bit of class. Inviting any more people from work inevitably opens up new chains of invitations (e.g., "If I invite Chucky from accounting, I have to invite Clarabelle from engineering; and if I invite Clarabelle, I have to invite Big Larry from collections; and so on and so on). Before you know it, your wedding has turned into the annual sales conference, and you're neither having fun, nor scoring any points with the brass down at the store. This whole category is an easy cut. Make it.

Screen #3: Cut the Kissing Cousins

This is another place where you can cut lots of people you hardly know without ruffling too many feathers. Keep the list of relatives down to first cousins, aunts, uncles, and grandparents. If you are one of those rare birds who are close to your second cousins, this becomes a tougher judgment call. Inviting a few of them starts another one of those invitee chains you're trying so hard to avoid. Try this: invite a cousin you really like, but ask him to come to the reception disguised in novelty-store Groucho glasses and a fright wig. That way, the relatives who would rat you out to your other cousins won't recognize him. Clever, huh? (If any of your other guests object to being seated at his table, tell them that your cousin poses no threat when he's taking his medication. In fact, why not seat a bunch of people you don't like too much at that table. They'll find some lame excuse to cut out early and, before you can say "Jack Robinson," it's more cake for everyone.)

Screen #4: Cut the Plus Ones

Now we're getting to some of the cruelest cuts—the noninvites that will inflame your friends, alienate their girlfriends and boyfriends, and reveal you as someone who is getting in touch with his inner schmuck. If space is still really tight, the dates stay home. All of the dates stay home no matter how laid your friends might get if they bring the new squeeze to an emotionally charged and free-boozy event such as an old pal's wedding.

There are exceptions to the rule. You should allow members of the bridal party to bring a date. After shelling out money for bridesmaid dresses and rental tuxes and suffering the indignities of being dolled up like a bunch of Opryland Hotel stewards, they deserve to treat their lovers to a bit of fish and a glass of champagne. It is precisely the least you can do.

OK, so you bit the bullet and cut the boyfriends and girlfriends. Can you save more space on the list by crossing off the husbands, wives, and fiancées? No. How about the really, really annoying ones? Again, no. As far as weddings go, married and engaged couples are considered a Siamese unit. They come and go together until death or divorce doth them part. That means your old buddy's untamed shrew with dragon breath and medieval table manners sits right up there at the head table. You could break with tradition and not invite her anyway, but it will most likely be perceived as an insult to both your friend and his wife. Don't do it unless you intend it as such. The one area here where there's still a judgment call concerns friends with live-in lovers. In my book (check the cover if you must), these people are more committed than most engaged couples and ought to qualify as a mandatory invite. If you have someone in this category you really want to exclude, however, you could hide behind this technicality like the conniving hair-splitter you are rapidly becoming. (See, I told you this was going to get ugly.)

Screen #5: Cut the Paybacks

Just because a distant relative made you suffer through his wedding doesn't mean that you have to make him suffer through yours. This goes double for all sets of parents. Take a close look at the list, and cross off names that are there only because you and/or your parents were invited to their weddings. This not only helps get your numbers down but also may have the ancillary benefit of saving you from attending lots and lots of baptisms, bar mitzvahs, birthday parties, and other events as your lesser friends return the snub.

Screen #6: Cut the Morons

Now that you've run all the easier screens, two kinds of people should be left on the list: people you really want to share a life-enhancing event with and people you feel deeply obligated to invite. You may want to buck up and make room for the extra people or simply hope for a good outbreak of a particularly nasty flu sometime around your wedding day. If you really can't stretch it any further, try this: look at the people who you are inviting only because you feel like you have to. Chances are a few people on the list are, to put it delicately, somewhat less pleasant than a flatulent warthog with leprosy. Cut them. If you have to offend someone, it might as well be someone you don't like.

We Kind of Request Your Company

So you've run all the screens, smote the malodorous, and you still can't get down to the magic number. You thought about expanding the list, but you've already pawned your beloved saxophone, and you're hitting up against the wedding-hall-occupancy rating anyway. In such desperate circumstances, you may be tempted to fall back to the old tiered-invitation system. The way this works is that some of your more distant relatives and casual friends are only invited to the wedding ceremony while people you like more than them get the all-access passes. This system sucks like a turbocharged Hoover. Yeah, a few dowagers might be just as happy skipping the reception. To most people, however, this will be received as something less than a treat. When you get down to it, this approach is a formal way of saying, "We know we have to invite you and wouldn't mind a present, but it's not like we like you enough to give you a stuffed mushroom or anything." This is supposed to make them feel included?

Want to do it anyway? You will need to make up two sets of invitations: one for the wedding and one for the reception. Send the people you don't want to insult both invitations. For those people you intend to embarrass and offend simply omit the reception invitation. Then see if you can look at yourself in the mirror.

Preventing the Sneak Attack

As soon as you announce your engagement, a bunch of people you don't intend to invite will approach you in a way that makes it clear they are expecting an invitation. The best advice is to be firm with these people. Look them in the eye and explain that your wedding is going to be a rather small, intimate affair, and, while you would love to be able to have them there, you simply don't have space for anyone other than a few close relatives. You should also cross at the green, not in between. You should brush at least three times a day and never, ever eat a box of Krispy Kreams in one sitting. We both know that the real world doesn't work that way.

So here's what you do. When Little Miss Presumptuous starts asking what she should wear to the wedding, do anything you can to dodge the question. Look at your feet, change the subject, cover your mouth as if you're about to vomit and run to the men's room, whatever it takes. This usually averts a socially awkward moment for at least a little while. If that fails, you could always cave and invite the cretin instead of one of your good friends. But that would make you a pathetic wuss. The nobler option is to lie like a rug and blame the unfortunate situation on your fiancée and her mother. Say, "I've got to be honest, my future mother-in-law invited everyone she knows, so I had just three slots. I only get to invite my parents and myself. I would have invited you, but my parents are terminally ill and want to see me married before they die. I hope you can see it in your heart to understand." Make sure you throw in that "I've got to be honest" part so that they'll think you are being honest.

Touchy People and Other Pains in the Butt

There was a time when people knew how to behave themselves in public situations. Even people who deeply hated each other managed to maintain some semblance of decorum until a proper duel could be arranged. At least that's the way they tell it in all those tedious Merchant Ivory movies.

Nowadays, some people have a looser definition of appropriate social behavior. Some of these people may be your relatives, and some of them may decide that your wedding reception is just the occasion to settle their grievances with equally ungracious relatives. While this often makes for good improvisational theater, it does introduce a somewhat excessive note of drama to the occasion. It pays to address some of the more volatile situations well in advance of the big event.

Stepmonsters

If you or your fiancée is the product of a broken home (don't you just love that phrase?), wedding politics get considerably more difficult. It helps if your parents are grown-ups, but that doesn't always work out the way we want it to, now does it? If you have one of those deals where every family event turns into a full-out, claws-and-whiskers catfight between your mom and your stepmother, you have to deal with the situation before the fur flies. In most cases, a stern warning and tables at opposite ends of the room will suffice. If you really have a "Jerry Springer" episode on your hands, then your mom comes and your stepmother doesn't. Same for the dads, with the possible addition of armed security and a restraining order. Yeah, a lot of feelings will be hurt, but what are you going to do?

In less testy climes, you should make it a point to invite step-brothers and -sisters. Even if you don't really like them all that much, it helps keep the family peace if you can stomach their presence. Why not be big about it?

People You Have Slept With

Here's a fun moment. A few years back a beautiful, smart, and fun woman dumped you like a bad habit, immediately taking up with a guy who has much better prospects than you will ever have. Now she's been tossed aside by Joe Perfect, and you're getting married to someone even smarter, prettier, and more fun than she'll ever be. Wouldn't this be a perfect opportunity to rub a little salt in the wounds? You're damn straight it would be. So have yourself a party. Unless of course, your fiancée has any sort of problem with you using her wedding day to make a point to someone off whose breasts you used to lick whipped cream. Aww, forget I ever mentioned it, why would she have a problem with that? You wouldn't mind if that stallion your fiancée used to date was sitting on her side of the aisle, would you? You know, the one who used to make the little missus scream, "Take me, take me, you Hun!" It would be kind of fun to see them do the lambada together at your wedding, wouldn't it?

The Outsiders

Out-of-town relatives deserve special consideration largely because they are far less likely to attend than your close-by relatives are. That means that you get more presents per chicken dinner than any other category of invitee, save for the hospitalized, imprisoned, and agoraphobic. Unless your circles of family and friends are unusually hardy travelers, you can probably get away with expanding your out-of-town guest list to cover a healthy ratio of no-shows. And remember, when assembling your guest list, it isn't how many people you invite that counts. It's how many actually come.

On the flip side, out-of-town friends and relatives who do decide to make the trip are going to be a bit more high maintenance than most. These people are willing to put up with mangled luggage, airport shoe searches, and rental-counter purgatory just to see you take the fall. The least you can do is to try to make their stay as convenient and comfortable as possible.

To begin with, you are expected to help all your out-of-town guests find a place to crash. Unless you have an unusually large and comfortable pullout couch, this means you will have to look into a few of the local hotels. If you are having more than a couple of guests wing in for the big event, you may want to consider reserving a block of rooms at the local flophouse. Many hotels, not having met your family and friends, will actually offer group discounts for wedding parties. If you're holding your reception at a hotel ballroom, you should even have some extra leverage to negotiate a good deal on the rooms upstairs. This has the added advantage of making sure your alcoholic uncle Sven from the Twin Cities won't wrap his rental Buick around a fire hydrant after the reception.

Whether or not you're booking rooms, include a note with the out-of-town invitations that lists several hotel options at a few different price points. Make sure your note includes the rates (daily, not hourly, you miscreant) and a number they can call for reservations. Also, be sure to detail such special features as free HBO, magic fingers, and in-room, champagne-glass–shaped hot tubs. In addition to helping them sort through the options, this card also lets them know that you don't intend on footing their hotel bills. Given the price of mini-bar Wild Turkey, this step alone could save you something like $47 million. (And you only shelled out a few lousy bucks for this book. Was that a deal, or what?)

While you don't need to pay their travel bills, you should provide some entertainment for the out-of-towners. It is customary to invite them to the rehearsal dinner the night before your wedding. This gives them something to do, other than watching Spectravision porno flicks, and lets them know you appreciate their spending thousands of dollars and a perfectly good weekend to see you wed. That's worth a few shrimp at the Red Lobster, isn't it?

Finally, make sure that your out-of-town guests know how to navigate the local terrain. Provide directions to the rehearsal dinner, ceremony, and reception from the hotels where your guests are staying. You may even want to ask a friend to lead a mighty convoy from the hotels to the ceremony. Assuming, of course, that you have a friend who can be trusted to lead them to the ceremony and not a particularly promising race at the track.

CHAPTER 8

The Invitations

Now that you've figured out who to invite to your wedding, let's take a moment to talk about how you're going to invite them. Let's start with the obvious. Most of these guests will be your friends and family, people you see all the time. You could just tell them, right? I'm thinking that the rest of them probably have phone numbers. You could just give them a call. You might even want to get fancy and pick up a box or two of those "We're Having a Party" invites down at the Hallmark store. Make sense?

No, sir. No, how.

What you'll want to do is spend well over a thousand bucks printing up invitations, envelopes, reception cards, maps with directions to the reception, reply cards, reply envelopes, and a whole slurry of other literature. You'll want to cram it all in a big, rich envelope with lots of odd pieces of tissue and vellum. Then you'll want to throw in a lead sinker or two, just to make sure the whole package is expensive enough to mail. And as long as you've come this far, why not hire a professional calligrapher, for hundreds more dollars, to address each and every one of them envelopes all pretty-like. That's what you'll want to do, because that makes sense. It makes sense because . . . well, all the girls know why, and they certainly aren't telling you if you don't already know. So just be still and keep licking those envelopes.

Paper Goods

There are only two other ways to make paper more expensive than wedding invitations. You could take it to your local mint and have them print c-notes on it, or you could have an artist of international repute sketch a donkey or something. These two unlikely scenarios aside, wedding invitations pretty much top the list.

If you want to spend more money on paper than you would on a perfectly serviceable dirt bike, settle for nothing less than real engraved invitations. To produce an engraved invitation, a printer must first cast a special metal plate. This is used to stamp the paper from behind, raising the letters off of the paper as the invitations are printed. If you ever want to tell if an invitation is really engraved, look at the back. The letters will be dented into the paper. All the more modern forms of pseudo-engraving will only raise the letters on the front. If mailing dented paper is the kind of thing that is important to you, you'll have to track down a local printer that still works the old-fashioned way. In some places, this may be hard to find. Engraving is a slowly dying art kept alive by insane people.

The next step down the wedding invitation food chain is thermography. Thermography is a printing process that heats up ink to create a raised letter effect similar to engraving. However, it is a whole lot cheaper, since there is no metal plate to create.

Thermography is almost certainly the kind of printing that will be used to produce your invitations. This is because almost all the major manufacturers of wedding invitations use it for almost all of their output. You will probably end up buying from one of these mighty cartels mostly because you have little choice. When you go down to the local stationery store to pick out the invites (given, of course, that it's you going), you will be shown a few catalogs from one or more of these world-league power brokers. They will have virtually any size, style, typeface, paper stock, color, and decorative embellishment that any right-minded person could possibly want. Yes, anything nice will be ugly expensive, but not nearly so ugly expensive as having your local printer re-create the wheel.

Some of you risk-loving, life-on-the-edge caballeros will not be happy with the status quo. Defying all social convention, you'll want to do something fun and whimsical and completely your own. You'll want your invitations to look like a concert poster from the old Filmore East. You'll want your invitations to feature that nude sketch you made of your fiancée in art school. Offset printing is the process for a man of your maverick ways. This is how virtually everything you ever read is printed. It's flat, flexible, cheap, and can be made to bend to your will. If you want to go your own route, take down the local yellow pages and let your fingers strut through the printer section. The stationery stores will most likely not be able to help.

Finally, there are those stoic sorts who will insist on hand lettering each and every one of their invitations. This is acceptable in social circles if you have very nice handwriting, particularly if you have studied calligraphy. It is not advisable if you are inviting hundreds of people to your wedding, or if your name is Jean-Michael Beauregard Smithington-Cauldwell, Junior, and you're marrying someone named Mary-Catherine Constantinople Worthington-Applewhite from East Outer Kalamazoo, Michigan. If you still want the hand-lettered look, help is on the horizon. Some mechanical processes approximate hand calligraphy. If you are into that sort of thing, ask your local stationer.

What Should It Say?

You can purchase etiquette guides with more than two-dozen right-and-proper ways to phrase a wedding invitation. You will find casual, formal, and downright stuffy variations. There is proscribed language for every major religion and more than a couple of lunatic fringe sects. There is different language based on how many parents are involved and how married and/or alive each one of them is. Since your fiancée already owns one of those books and is going to just tell you what yours will say, let's cut this short. Here's one all-purpose wedding invitation:

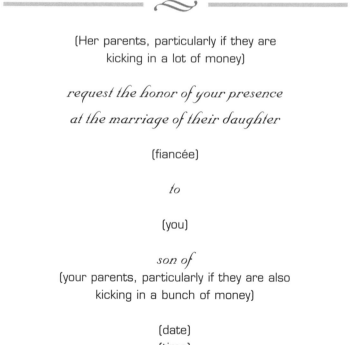

(Her parents, particularly if they are
kicking in a lot of money)

request the honor of your presence

at the marriage of their daughter

(fiancée)

to

(you)

son of
(your parents, particularly if they are also
kicking in a bunch of money)

(date)
(time)
(place)
(city, state)

Of course, that would be the kind of all-purpose invitation used by all those workaday drudges who lack your individualistic flare. You'll want to strike out on your own here, right? Maybe pen a little love poem or otherwise use this as an opportunity to tell the world why you are marrying each other. Before you get carried away, remember that this invitation will be sent to your brothers, your bowling team, and your sarcastic cousin Ernest. Any mention of "uniting spirits for all eternity," or "helping us celebrate a love that only now dares to speak its name" can and should be severely mocked.

Likewise, be really cautious about adding too many visual elements to your invitations. If you want to show two horses tied to a rail with a caption reading "We're gettin' hitched," I personally would be glad to join you at Cracker Barrel for your reception. Less open-minded souls than I, however, might well assume you are marrying a first cousin. Pictures of you and your spouse are less tacky. Just not enough less.

One note of caution: a wedding invitation is a really crappy place to take revenge on your family. If your parents are divorced and your dad is a jerk, you both might be tempted to list your mom and cool stepfather as the sponsors of the wedding. This is a sixteen-gauge gut-shot insult to your father played out before all of your acquaintances. Don't do it. If you do, don't expect him to pop for that swank Limoges sugar and creamer set you registered for.

Shipping and Handling

Once you've picked out stock and style, settled on language, and determined a quantity, it's time to place your order. This should be done approximately three months ahead of D day, longer if you are going the engraved route. When placing the order, make sure you proofread each and every line as closely as you possibly can. If your fiancée's name is Joan, for example, you don't want to send out invitations saying that you're marrying someone named "John." (Not that there's anything wrong with that.)

Speaking of mistakes, make sure that you order enough extra envelopes to screw up regularly. Print up about 5 to 10 percent more invitations than you think you'll need, and 10 to 15 percent more envelopes. It's usually pretty cheap to throw in a few extra in your initial order. If you have to go back and order more later, it's like starting all over again. Believe me, you are going to need most of the extras. Addressing invitations is one of the most mind-numbing, arm-aching chores you are ever likely to encounter. Consider yourself lucky if you are blessed with barely legible chicken scratch writing. If not, fake it. If you can't get away with that, buy a good bottle of bourbon and invite some friends with nice penmanship to a little addressing party. Just make sure you mete out the Wild Turkey judiciously. You are likely in for some long nights. For each invitation, you have to hand address an outer envelope, an inner envelope, and a reply envelope.

Couldn't you just hire someone to do this? Yes, but your fiancée might insist on this being a professional calligrapher. Depending on how many people you are inviting, that could set you back the cost of a decent camcorder. Depending on whether or not you actually have to do any of the work, it may well be worth it.

Neither Rain, nor Sleet, nor Snow . . .

So, your invitations are printed, the envelopes are addressed, and a truly bizarre pile of envelopes and enclosures have been neatly stuffed into large, heavy envelopes. Before you stick them in the mail, take a few samples down to the post office and have them weighed. The last thing you want is to have the whole mess coming back at you because of insufficient postage. Besides, it's always amusing to find out how much it costs to ship phone book–sized envelopes all over the country. While you're at it, make sure to buy stamps for all of the reply envelopes. You know that rich uncle of yours with the ski house in Aspen you've never been invited to? You sure wouldn't want him spending a few dimes on a stamp, now would you?

Be sure that you have the whole pile in the mail about eight weeks before the wedding. That way you'll be able to get all the RSVPs back in time to turn in numbers to your caterers. Sure, a whole bunch of your motley crew will not be able to figure out what a reply envelope might be used for. Wait two weeks and give them a call. After that, send a collection agency after them.

With that, at least you're all finished with the costly and time-consuming printing business, right? Right, as soon as you polish off the thank-you notes, engagement announcements, ceremony programs, and reception place cards.

Hey, no one said this was going to be easy.

CHAPTER 9

The Bridal Party

In case you've never been outside the Hollow, a bridal party is the supporting cast of a traditional wedding. There are supporting roles for a best man and a maid of honor, a longer chorus line of bridesmaids and groomsmen, and a few character bits for a flower girl and a ring bearer. Your bride, yourself, and the officiant who marries you are also considered part of the bridal party, but we're not worried about you all right now. You have enough on your hands trying to cast the rest of these parts.

Selecting your bridal party is kind of like the guest list thing on steroids. Unless you're fortunate enough to be a truly unlikable human being with few friends and no family, you may have a tough time choosing sides for the big game. This is because, despite the fact that these people will have jobs to do, choosing a bridal party is mostly a way of telling your family and friends which of them means the most to you. You may not intend it as such, but it will nearly always be taken that way. Telling an old bud that you really wanted him to be an usher but were afraid he couldn't point to a chair with the same panache as your other pals just ain't gonna cut the Grey Poupon. Get used to it now. Unless the math gods love you, you are probably going to piss off a good friend or two when your bridal party cast list is posted. They may have enough class to keep it a secret, but someone will be pissed.

According to tradition, it is your job to select the best man and groomsmen, while your bride picks the maid of honor and bridesmaids. Of course, these traditions were established when it was considered unseemly for an unwed person to have friends of the opposite sex. Nowadays, it tends to work more like a court appointment. If you have a female friend or sister who you would like in the bridal party, you make the nomination. Your fiancée reviews her application, perhaps calls her before the committee for interrogation, then either confirms or denies the candidate. Likewise, if she has a brother or male friend she wants in the bridal party, she tells you and you just do it. (Even if you can't stand the little SOB, offer to make him an usher. Just make sure that he understands that flying-nature wedgies are part of the groomsman-initiation process and that all the other guys have already been through it.)

Particularly left-brain kinds of brides might insist that the bridal party consist of equal numbers of bridesmaids and groomsmen. This has several benefits. First, it makes for nice symmetrical pictures, particularly if you cast friends and family of the correctly ascending heights. It also makes for uniformly hetero couples promenading down the aisle ahead of the bride. Most important, an equal number of bridesmaids and ushers create a higher degree of difficulty in the selection process. Now you need an equal number of male and female friends and/or family that you would like to honor and/or snub. All of this wedding plan stuff was probably going a little too easy, and you needed a tough one to wake you up a bit, now didn't you?

If you are really having trouble balancing the wedding party, you may want to create a few extra gigs to accommodate those friends still left out in the cold. For example, you could have a couple of friends read some nice passages during the ceremony. If you have an unusually talented musician in your circle, perhaps he or she could whistle a tune or play the kazoo as you walk the aisle. As for more practical positions—like bouncer, bathroom steward, and hat-check girl—it's really best to leave these jobs to the pros.

The Best Man

All those books your fiancée is reading will tell you that the best man has important responsibilities, so you shouldn't just pick your best friend or favorite brother. So what you should do is pick your best friend or favorite brother. The other guys can help him with his indispensably important duties, and managing to make a ring stay in your pocket is not exactly rocket science. More than anything else, asking someone to be your best man is a compliment. It's saying, you're the Butch to my Sundance, the Abbott to my Costello, the Tonto to my Lone Ranger. But not meaning it in a gay way or anything.

Of course, many of us have a couple of old friends and/or brothers who fit the bill. If one doesn't step out of the pack, making the call gets a bit tougher. Here's how you should make the cut: the only thing a best man has to do that can't be done by a mentally handicapped Labrador retriever is give a speech at your reception. So forget about the best man for a minute, and just go pick a bunch of guys to be your groomsmen. From this motley crew, decide who is most likely to give a good speech, and ask him to be your best man. Tell all the others that you chose that guy because he was feeling down in the dumps about being a thirty-year-old bed wetter and you thought he could use a nice little pick-me-up.

Of course, the other major responsibility of the best man is to organize your bachelor party. You might use this task as a check on the selection process. If the best speaker among your buds is likely to get you all thrown in jail the night of your bachelor party, you might want to briefly consider whether or not he has the bail-bond connections to get you out before the wedding. Alternately, pick a marginally more responsible friend to be your best man.

Beyond the speech and the party, your best man is also charged with pocketing the wedding rings during the ceremony and handing them over when needed. He has to wear what you ask him to and pay for it no matter how much it costs and how silly it looks. He can be asked to hand out checks to the various service providers. Your best man is also charged with getting you to the church on time. Sober. If you want to throw something else on the list, go ahead. Tell him that the traditional duties of a best man include washing your car, expressing your dog's anal glands, and carrying your bag whenever you play golf together for the rest of your lives. Who knows? He might just fall for it.

The Second-Best Men

The ushers and groomsmen are all of the guys who didn't quite make the cut as your best man. Fortunately, they have a pretty simple gig. They have to show up in the clothes you asked them to wear and escort your guests to their seats without tripping or saying anything too stupid. They may also be called on to light church candles, roll out an aisle runner, carry gifts to a secure location, and perform other menial tasks. Basically, anyone who can tie his shoes, walk a few yards, and understand the English words *bride* and *groom* should be up to the task. If you can't find a half-dozen or so guys who can step up to the challenge, don't worry. The church or synagogue could probably lend you a few guys from the maintenance staff for the afternoon.

Of course, all of this is only the paper definition of the groomsman position. The real role of your groomsmen is to help give an air of roguish, good humor to the event. Your groomsmen will be expected to drink liberally without getting too sloppy or starting any fights. They should dance exuberantly, if not necessarily well. The single guys are expected to make a pass at a few of the single female guests, preferably a bridesmaid or two. In fact if one of them hooks up with his future wife at your reception, all the better. Mostly, the chummy camaraderie of your ushering cadre helps convince all your new in-laws of what a swell guy you are.

Of course, the line between rogue and vandal is awfully fine and difficult to see after an evening-long tango with Jose Cuervo. Depending on the fitness, character, and rap sheets of your groomsmen, you may want to take a few simple precautions. Don't tell them where you parked your car. Don't tell them where you are spending your wedding night. Don't make it easy for them to follow you. That playful, practical-jokey humor that was so charming at the reception gets really unfunny outside your hotel door at 2 A.M., just as the missus is about to unveil that new lingerie she bought for your first romp as husband and wife.

The Bridesmaids

You only need to know three things about bridesmaids:

1. You have to be nice to them no matter how much time they have spent trying to make your wife realize that deep down, underneath it all you really are an asshole.
2. You love the dresses your wife picked out for them, and, yes, unlike every bridesmaid dress that has come before, they really will be able to wear them again and again and again and again.
3. No matter how inexplicably sexy they may look in their outlandishly poofy dresses, you can't sleep with bridesmaids anymore. Sorry.

The Maid of Honor

Same as the above, only more so. Especially #3.

The Cherubs

Your most junior attendants come in four flavors: junior bridesmaid, flower girl, ring bearer, and trainbearer (aka *page*). Due to the general shortage of good-looking children, and the child labor laws in most states, these positions are considered optional. However, if you have some youngins in the family who you are particularly fond of, you may want to consider suiting a couple of them up. They can be awfully cute when they're spiffed up, and it's nice getting that big "aaawwww" when the little guys appear in the aisle.

Junior bridesmaid is a title conferred upon little Britneys from about ten to fourteen years old. It allows them to be a bridesmaid until 9 P.M. and only when accompanied by a senior bridesmaid. OK, they really do the same thing as the other bridesmaids. They just give them a different title so as not to confuse the groomsmen.

Trainbearers have the most difficult task of any of the kids involved in your wedding. (Unless you count all the third-world children who put in eighty-hour weeks making those plastic bride-and-groom cake toppers we've all just got to have.) The job is to follow the bride down the aisle, holding the long train of her dress . . . without picking it up and looking at her underwear. Sure, this would be easy enough if you hired on a couple of cute little girls to handle the task. But this gig traditionally goes to prepubescent boys. You know, the kind of humans who think that there is no greater stroke of luck than to find a six-month-old *Playboy* in someone's garbage. Asking them to walk fifty feet holding the back of a girl's dress without taking a peek is more than a mild form of torture. And here's the real kicker: You may have to find two boys equal to the task. Much like Jell-O shots, trainbearers are thought to work better in pairs.

The much sought-after ring bearer position also usually goes to a little boy, although no federal statutes dictate that a man cub must perform the job. That would be unconstitutional. For some reason that no one understands, the ring bearer proceeds down the aisle carrying two fake rings tied to a little doily-encrusted pillow. He totes this all the way up front and hands it to the best man, who has the real rings in his pocket all along. Oddly, this is not considered a cruel joke.

The flower girl generally enjoys her part more than the ring bearer because, hey, little girls are just like that. Her job is to walk down the aisle immediately before the bride, spreading a thick mat of slippery flower petals on the slick silk runner. She is to look cute doing this. Oddly, it is not considered an act of mischief if the bride, in her shiny new shoes, slips on the pedals and goes crashing into the lap of Uncle Waldo from Dubuque.

Kids get away with the coolest stuff nowadays.

Paying the Posse

It is customary for the bride and groom to give thank-you presents to members of their bridal party. Theoretically, all of these presents come from both you and your bride, so you should share in the selection process, even for all the bridesmaids' presents. Believe me, no one wants this. Let's just keep this simple. The same rules apply to bridesmaid presents as applied for dresses. No matter what lame-ass tchotchke she picks out for the ladies, you love it. You know deep in your soul that the bridesmaids will love it, cherish it, and come to rely on it like nothing else. Your intended has probably put a bizarre amount of thought into those earrings, or whatever, and the last thing she needs is your brain-dead opinion on the subject. The same thing holds for the presents for your parents. She'll probably pick out a couple of nice picture frames or something. You'll love them, yadda, yadda, yadda.

As for your groomsmen, your fiancée may point to a helpful passage in her wedding guide that says something like this:

Great Gifts for Groomsmen
◆ Money clips
◆ Date books
◆ Cologne
◆ Silk ties
◆ Key rings
◆ Travel or shaving kits

When she does, point to this list:

Gifts for Groomsmen That Suck
◆ Money clips
◆ Date books
◆ Cologne
◆ Silk ties
◆ Key rings
◆ Travel or shaving kits

After you do that, make sure she doesn't read any further so she won't know what you're really going to get them until it's too late. In fact, whatever it is that you're going to buy, have it monogrammed so it can't be returned. (Unless you get them something like cheese. Monogramming that would be disgusting.)

Now, if you really want to do this right, you will think long and hard about what each of your friends would truly treasure. You would consider your friends' professions, hobbies, and interests. You would contemplate the times you have spent together; perhaps that would provide a clue for exactly the right gift. After really thinking it through, you might just come to the realization that you have become . . . well . . . a girl. Yeah, I know. What you are really going to do is stop by a store on your way home from work one night, point to one cool thing and say, "Can you monogram six of those?"

Here are some cool things to point at:

◆ Hip flasks
◆ Professional-grade corkscrews

- Premium hooch and/or stogies
- Shiny electronic gadgets
- Sophisticated paint-ball weaponry
- Ball-game tickets
- Anything that makes an undue amount of noise and/or sawdust

CHAPTER 10

The Reception Hall

Welcome to the section where your family fortunes start taking a turn for the worse. And not just a tad worse. I'm talking something-out-of-a-Steinbeck-novel worse. I'm talking strap-the-few-remaining-dust-encrusted-family-possessions-to-the-broken-down-pickup-and-follow-the-harvest-to-California worse. This is because you, my little buddy, are about to go looking for a room big enough to hold your reception.

"So, why the dramatics, Wedding Dude?" I hear you scoff. Well, scoff away, dear boy, and we'll see who has the last scoff here. Right now, you're thinking it won't be such a big deal to book a room, aren't ya? What do a fella and his best gal really need to hold a wingding of a wedding? Four walls, one roof, and a couple latrines, preferably with indoor plumbing. So the family wants a little class. You're down with that. A little marble here, a couple of Liberace-esque candelabra strewn about, perhaps some chintz. (Never mind that neither of us really knows what chintz is, it sure sounds classy.) Why, you shall be wed in a hall for the ages. How much could a simple little thing like that cost?

$84 million. Give or take.

That's approximately $84 million before you add tax, tip, and allowances for all those silly champagne flutes your ushers are going to break. And that's $84 million American. If you think you're getting the Canadian discount in this realm, Dudley DoRight, don't even think aboot it!

How to Rent a Room by the Hour

Before you and your beloved intended go running willy-nilly about town looking at every flea-bitten joint that can hold your extended posse, it makes sense to sit down and talk about what kind of general setting you had in mind. So, put your willy down, slip that nilly back in its scabbard, and have yourselves a little heart to heart. You may want to get the ball rolling by expressing your fondness for something a little simpler and more casual. Maybe something like the local off-track betting parlor. You've been to some swell affairs (a word to use cautiously around your future wife) there and always kind of liked the blue-collar ambience. Or hey, wouldn't it be kind of neat to just take over the pool hall/bowling alley/video arcade for the night? You could hand out quarters to everyone and have someone in to show some trick shots. "Wouldn't that be fun, dear? Whatta ya say?!"

The best way to get the swelling down on that shiner is to grab a big old Fred Flintstone–size steak out of the freezer and slap it right on. You might also want to pop a few Advil and continue this discussion in a more adult manner in the morning.

If you're still reading, I'm guessing the little lady and her retinue are looking for a, shall we say, somewhat more traditional venue. Just to give you a taste of what you're in for here, basically, you'll be checking out two kinds of places. First, you'll investigate the places that exist primarily to host wedding receptions and other banquets: hotel ballrooms, country clubs, and wedding factories. Certain larger restaurants also fall into this category. The nice part about going this route is that these venues will have someone there who has helped more people organize their weddings than a barrel full of Sun Young Moons. Second, you'll look into the nontraditional wedding sites, such as zoos, museums, or jai alai stadiums.

If you choose one of the big wedding venues, you can expect them to have all the options laid out for you. You (meaning your fiancée and her mother) pretty much just assemble the reception like you're ordering for the table at Lucky Chow's Chinese Restaurant and Polynesian Lounge. (Which I would highly recommend for your wedding if you can get away with it. Just stay away from the moo goo gai pan.) The downside is that:

- It will be expensive.
- You'll have to book way ahead of time; way, way ahead of time; or way, way, way ahead of time.
- There's a certain been-there, done-that quality to all of these places.

I'm not advocating against the traditional sites. Some are beautiful. Some are comically tacky. All of them will make the next year of your life considerably easier than it will be if you book a place that doesn't routinely host weddings.

The Reception Less Traveled

So you couldn't just take the easy way out, could you? Well, welcome to the big wide world, Tenderfoot. Let's see what else is out there. Here are some places that could be substantially cooler than a wedding factory, yet still not be masochistically inconvenient:

- Fancy pants manor houses and historic properties
- Museums and galleries (bonus points if you can talk her into a wax museum)
- Zoos and aquariums (avoid close proximity to the monkey house)
- Parks, greenhouses, and botanical gardens (saves bunches of bucks on flowers)
- Booze cruise boats, yachts, and other boozy floating places
- Theaters and concert halls (very dramatic)
- College chapels and courtyards (as if they'd let you back there)
- Ski lodges (extra credit for the lodge at the summit)
- Beaches, mountain passes, and other scenic wonders

Will these places be more charming than booking Mister Maxwell's Wedding Emporium conveniently located by the exit to the interstate? Of course they will. Will it be more trouble? Yeah, probably. You're most likely looking at trucking in your own caterer; renting tents, chairs, and tables; working out some logistical wrinkles with the band or DJ; and maybe hassling with city hall to get the right permits. If you go this route, you may want to limit your choices to places that have pulled off at least a couple of weddings before. They will have learned from somebody else's mistakes and probably will have the basic logistics worked out. You should also consider hiring a caterer who has thrown at least a party or two there before. In these sorts of venues, local experience really counts.

The extreme version of the above is to hold the wedding at someone's house. Rent *The Father of the Bride*, both the Spencer Tracy and Steve Martin versions, and make the owner of the house watch them before he or she consents. Make them watch twice if you plan to have more than forty or fifty people.

For those of you who find even these sorts of venues too banal, the sky is not necessarily the limit. Just remember that a lot of venues seem like good fun until someone puts an eye out. Think hard before booking:

- Amusement parks, go-cart tracks, mini-golf courses, and the like
- Underwater, skydiving, hot-air ballooning, or otherwise lofty sites
- Flat out weird Goth places that give the rest of us the creeps
- Clothing-optional venues, particularly if your family is not unusually attractive

When the Hunter Becomes the Prey

So you've narrowed the field and are ready to go look at some rooms. You are going to be slamming down some serious jack here, so make sure you ask the tough questions before they officially have you by the jewels.

Here are some tough questions to throw at whomever is in charge of the place:

- How many drunken revelers does the room hold?
- Do you pour cheap, watered-down well booze into fancy bottles and try to pass it off as the real stuff?
- Are you willing to prove it by pouring us a free Johnny Walker Black right now? (And a person can't tell these things by just one sip, ya know?)
- Will you get all huffy if our Greek friends get carried away and bust up most of the crockery?
- How many health department violations has your on-site caterer had in the last six months?
- Will we be allowed to bring in our own caterer in the event that

1. Your guys can't pull off the traditional Mongolian Goat Roast we've always dreamed of, or,
2. Yours sucks.

◆ Do you have multiple reception sites, and if so, how many functions will be going on at the same time?
◆ Will any of those other functions be either a high school prom or a Hell's Angels family picnic?
◆ If the food is better at one of those other receptions, can we have a bite?
◆ What are the charges for doormen, coat check, valet parkers, and the other glam boys?
◆ What are the time limits, and what happens if we inform the powers that be that we are going over?
◆ If my fiancée finally gets some sense in her head and calls this thing off, do I get my money back?
◆ If you won't give the cash back, will you at least make it up in leftover crab puffs and chopped liver swan sculptures?

I hope I don't have to remind you that you should be asking these questions at a minimum of three or four places before making any decisions. Narrow the field too early and you are primed to be fleeced like a New Zealand lamb. In fact, some couples go to dozens of venues before making the cut, but they are mostly just in it for the free hors d'oeuvres. Make sure to take good notes so that you can remember what you liked and didn't like about each venue you visited. A guy like you is likely to get a bit confused after you've visited, let's say, two of these places. The notes will help you keep track of who said what.

Once you've narrowed the field, it's a good idea to drop by some night when a reception is in progress and snoop around a little. If everything looks reasonably clean and orderly, and the people look happy, it's probably OK. Dress appropriately, and you can probably even get free cake. You should also talk to several people who've held a reception there, preferably people whose names weren't supplied by the site.

If you're feeling comfortable with your pick, get them to write down all of the numbers. And make sure to stress *all*. Things like sales tax and mandatory tips can add up to 25 percent to the bottom line. Plus, some places throw in charges for parking and coat check and bathroom attendants and everyone else who's ever had a job there. Make sure you understand what happens if you have to adjust your guest list up or down at the last minute. Also make sure that your rates are locked in, particularly if you are booking way ahead of time. You don't want to get stuck paying next year's rates. Bottom line, make sure you and your fiancée read and understand everything before signing the contract. Like I said, there's a lot of money on those tables.

The Food and Drink

When you invite people to your wedding reception, they will expect to be fed. People are just funny that way. You will definitely appear to be the more gracious host if you put out something for them to eat. Something like an extensive raw bar elaborately cascading about a carved ice swan, a self-contained universe of hors d'oeuvres orbiting the hall on silver-esque trays, all followed by a full eight-course meal. Oh yeah, they'll want something to drink with that, too.

Want a quick idea of what you're in for? Think for a moment about the last time you took your fiancée out for a really nice dinner. Not a regular Saturday night kind of nice dinner but a very special occasion nice dinner. The kind of dinner you might only have sprung for once in your life, because in a moment of generous tenderness you realized that it would substantially increase your chances of getting lucky that night. Remember all the cocktails you had at the bar and the nice bottle of wine you bought to impress her. (By the way, it's only impressive if you can pronounce the name, Slick.) The dessert was fabulous, wasn't it? Feeling a little expansive that night you quadrupled your customary 5 percent tip. You were likely too drunk to notice the 8 percent restaurant tax. Now close your eyes and picture this. The waiter is coming back with that leatherette folder with the AmEx logo. Your credit card sticks out of the side in that silly little plastic sleeve. That little piece of paper you signed, picture the number you just wrote in above your John Hancock. Got it? Good.

Now divide that by two, and multiply it by the number of people you expect at your reception. Not pretty, is it? In fact, for anyone who has ever hesitated to pick up a check for more than a few people, the catering bill for your reception is going to come as a shocker.

Someone's in the Kitchen with Your Credit Card

When it comes to slopping the masses at your wedding reception, there are basically two ways to go. You can use the in-house caterer at the venue you have selected, or you can bring someone in from the outside. Sometimes, this choice is made for you. Many country clubs, hotels, and other popular wedding spots don't allow competing caterers on their turf. Try it, and you'll incite a rumble like you haven't seen since the last revival of *West Side Story*. On the other hand, you may also have chosen a reception site that doesn't have an in-house caterer. Unless you plan on tossing out Snack-ems and Cracker Jack, you're going to have to bring someone in. For now, let's assume you have a choice.

The in-house caterer is often the smart choice because everyone starts with the same understanding. From the word *go*, everyone knows he has you by the balls, so there is no confusion. With an outside caterer, you often don't discover that he has you by the balls until the day of your reception, and that could easily sour your mood. Who needs that?

The in-house caterer provides other advantages. He or she obviously knows the room pretty well and might have a better sense of how to set it up. All the linens and things are there, and the caterer is not afraid to use them. The greatest advantage, however, is that you won't have to go sample every chicken kabob within a twenty-five-mile radius looking for someone else.

On the downside, the in-house guy knows he has the edge and is not likely to give it away for free. This may not be the most expensive option of all the caterers you'll find, but it sure ain't going to be the cheapest either. It's also possible that the in-house caterer, despite all of his or her boyish and/or girlish charm, sucks at cooking. In some extreme cases, this will have a direct impact on the quality of your meal. How can you tell? Hmmm. You could write the Culinary Institute of America to see if he has ever been dragged before the peer review board for butchering a soufflé, or you could taste the food. Whatever seems to make more sense for your personal style.

Outside caterers come in many flavors. (Sorry, I couldn't help myself.) Basically, however, they fall into two categories: those who are good at cooking, and those who are bad at cooking. To go way out on a limb here, I'm going to recommend that you go with the ones who are good at cooking. I don't mean to cast any aspersions on the bad-at-cooking caterer. Good at cooking is just my personal preference in someone who prepares food for me.

If you need some help sorting caterers into lists of good and bad at cooking, I would recommend you follow the same procedure you used to determine the quality of the in-house caterer's fare.

Now that you've compiled a nice assortment of caterers who excel at cooking, you may want to sort this group into two piles. In the first, put caterers you can afford. In the second put caterers you can't afford. Like many of us, you might just discover that the first pile is a whole lot smaller than the second one. In fact, if that first pile is an army of one, congratulations! You've just found your caterer. If a few contenders are still clawing it out, let's see if we can't separate the he-men from the boys. You will do this by asking the following questions:

- Do you have any food-related felony convictions? (This question accomplishes nothing except to put your caterer off guard, thus giving you the upper hand.)
- What is the absolute final, pinch-me-if-I'm-wrong food price? (In some cases the difference between the estimated food price and the actual food price is roughly akin to the difference between fantasy and reality. If you are booking a caterer way ahead of the event, he may want to leave a little wiggle room for escalating food prices. Fair enough. Just get a firm date for when the caterer must provide a firm price. Make certain that date is far enough in advance of the wedding to properly smack the little twit if he tries something cute.)
- What are the options in terms of serving the food? Buffet? Sit-down? Stadium-style Cracker Jack hurling? How many unemployed actors will you deploy in these efforts? Will these embittered showgirls be passing out hors d'oeuvres or just standing in the corner watching your guests cluster around the table like hogs at the trough?
- How much will we be required to tip these perky little *Variety* subscribers?
- Are you properly equipped and insured to pour hooch?
- Can you arrange a DJ, a cake, a photographer, and anything else we feel like throwing at you because we're getting sick of this and want somebody else to deal with it?
- Let's say one of us were to be caught in *flagrente delecto* with a, oh, a Tijuana hooker named Jezebel, you know, theoretically speaking. Oh hell, what's your cancellation policy?

◆ Who put the ram in the ram-a-lam-a-ding-dong? Tell me! Tell me! Tell me, infidel!!! (Again, serving no purpose but to keep the upper hand.)

Booze, Glorious Booze

There was a time when you weren't considered legally married if your reception bar bill did not exceed the food bill. This time extended from the wine-swilling Greeks through the flagon-of-mead raising knights to the speak-easy flappers right on through to the three-martini, Eisenhower, country-club crowd. Then the government got involved and spoiled all the fun. Sure, drunken brawls are down at weddings, as are duels and swordplay. One drunken aunt is marginally less likely to spit in the eye of another precipitating a family spat that lasts until your children's wedding. Yeah, it's all a little saner now, but I kind of miss the good old days.

It's all gotten just a bit complicated. Back in the olden days, if a wedding guest got blotto and rammed his horse into a school carriage, it was considered to be his fault. That's all changed in this enlightened age of reason. Now, if your uncle Bill downs two or three six-packs in the traditional wedding beer funnel and runs over someone's pet schnauzer on the ride back home, it's your fault. It's also the caterer's fault, the brewer's fault, and most likely the fault of the companies that manufactured the components from which your bridal party assembled the funnel. As a result, you may well want to have a few taxis on call to shuttle home the liver impaired and have the valet institute a Breathalyzer test before returning anyone's keys. Such is life in the third millennium.

Liability would be the first reason for putting some kind of limit on the total alcohol consumption at your wedding. The second is cost. Booze, even cheap booze, can be soberingly expensive to serve at your wedding. If you want to do this the right and proper way, you will have champagne for toasts, wine with the meal, and an open bar for the duration of the reception. It will be real champagne (or at least some premium sparkling wine), fine wine, and premium hooch at the bar. This will cost an awful lot of money. Basically, you are walking into a very crowded bar and saying, "A round for everyone on me." Then you're going to the equally crowded bar next door and doing it again. Then again. And quite possibly again and again and again.

So what are you going to do to get the costs down and limit your liability? There are a few mildly acceptable solutions:

- **Serve cheap booze:** Just make sure it's not disgustingly cheap.
- **BYOB:** In some situations, you may be allowed to supply your own alcohol. If this is an option, you should definitely take advantage of it. The markup on booze is rather extreme, so you can save some serious jack even if you have to pay a modest corkage fee. Watch out for that one, however. Sometimes this caterer's BYOB tax can all but eliminate the savings.
- **Offer tray service:** Instead of an open bar, have the unemployed actors tote large trays of drinks. Wine and beer are popular choices, but you wouldn't go to jail if you insisted on Mud Slings, Grasshoppers, and Sloe Comfortable Screws.
- **Put only wine out on the tables:** Yeah, if it's good wine and you keep putting it out, it could suffice. It's just a bit tough on those who don't like wine much. For some of the guests who are more set in their ways, it just ain't a party if they can't knock back a bourbon or two.
- **Close the bar early:** Shutting down the bar an hour or two before the end of the wedding could trim the costs and help people sober up before they drive home. Just make sure you line up a few rounds for yourself before they do.
- **Have a cash bar:** Some advocate for having guests pay for their own drinks. I agree. In fact, why not have them pay for their own meal. And where do they get off attending your ceremony for free? You should charge at least $10 admission and sell bags of rice for $3.50 a pop on their

way out the door. No, sir. No way. Cash bars at weddings are an appalling and insulting practice. If you can't afford an open bar, buy a keg of Genessee Cream Ale and a couple jugs of Riunite Lambrusco.

Know When to Say When

Just because you are paying for all the drinks doesn't mean you should be trying to get your fair share. If you are one of those guys who tends to pound down a few quick ones when he gets excited, make sure you go a bit slow at your reception. At the very least, follow every drink with a full glass of water and shy away from salty foods. Remember that you may well get too busy to do a lot of eating. So those eight rounds of toasts and a few shots of tequila with the boys at the bar could hit you like a locomotive. Go too far and you have a fantastic opportunity to embarrass yourself in front of a combined assembly of all your family and friends. But why should your wedding night be different? That's not what's at stake here. Remember, your fiancée has spent many, many hours selecting exactly what lingerie she will debut this evening. She has plans for the likes of you. You will need your wits about you.

CHAPTER 12

The Vows

When we start bellyaching about all the difficulties of planning our weddings, most of us aren't actually talking about our weddings. We're talking about our wedding *receptions*, the mere celebration of the fact we were married. Fortunately, by virtue of tradition and culture, planning the ceremony is usually the easier part.

Except when it isn't.

How much time and effort you put into planning your actual ceremony will depend largely on how literally you subscribe to tenets of your religion. If you are a member of a religious congregation, and are marrying someone of the same faith, you're strutting down Easy Street. Most religions have some pretty solid ideas about how their folks ought to get hitched. In fact, many religions leave exceptionally little to the imagination. Sure, you get to pick some processional music, decide where to put the flower baskets, and maybe even select a reading or two. Everything else, however, is done by the book. God has told you who should say what when. He or She has laid down the law on when to stand, when to sit, when to take up serpents, and when to writhe on the floor speaking in tongues. Who are you to argue?

As long as we're making this easy for ourselves, let's assume that you and the little lady are high school sweethearts who fell in love that crazy summer the church youth group held its work camp on the Indian reservation. (That bingo parlor sure did need sprucing up, didn't it?) You should be virtually home free ceremony-wise. You already know what church, temple, or druid ruin you are getting married in and who will be doing the officiating.

So, rather than going into the specifics of all the various religious services, let's just agree that you will ask your local priest/chaplain/minister/rabbi/priestess how the particulars work in your sect. This is one of those times in life when you hope you don't run into a practical joker. The possibilities here are virtually endless.

Likewise, if you are a godless heathen, and are marrying someone equally destined for H-E-double toothpicks, you are likely to have an easier time reaching an agreement on how your ceremony should proceed. This is particularly true if both of you don't want to make a big show of the ceremony before you bring out the satanic band. You will simply stand before a justice of the peace, judge, or notary public. After briefly reaffirming your belief in Darwinian theory of evolution and your deep, heartfelt opposition to prayer in school, you will be asked if your legal teams have reached a binding agreement. You will say "I do" with as little equivocation as your attorney allows. That's it. You are now free to progress toward a life of civilly sanctioned bliss. In these cases, you are most likely getting married wherever you hold your reception, so you save yourself the cost of a church. (If you don't count your everlasting soul as a cost.) As for the officiant—we'll get to that later.

Mixed Marriages

So you couldn't find a nice Jewish/Lutheran/Catholic/Druid girl from your local temple/congregation/parish/cult compound? Would that really have been so difficult? You actually placed the strength of her character, the power of her smile, the way she makes you feel like you own the world . . . all of those trivial concerns ahead of what book of worship she reads on Sunday morning?! Shame on you. To punish you, we are going to make your wedding ceremony very annoying and difficult to plan.

Today, mixed marriages come in more varieties than mixed drinks. In addition to your run-of-the-mill Protestant/Catholic and Jewish/Christian blends, you now commonly throw Muslims, Buddhists, Hindus, and godless atheists into the mix. Of course, each one of these religions has many sects and strains. Protestantism, in fact, has about fourteen billion sects, enough to handle the expanding world population through the next several centuries. On the upside, this means that the mechanisms for hitching up youngins who disappoint their parents have become much more robust. On the flip side, you are still pretty much going to have to make this up as you go along.

If you are of one faith, and your bride is of another, you need to have a frank discussion about which God you will be sacrificing your chickens to, and in which faith you will raise your future spawn. Will it be yours, hers, all of the above, or none of the above? Keep in mind that if you choose all of the above, you are likely to need a very large supply of candles, and you will be doing much more gift shopping for the rest of your life. In any case, I would use your answer to the above as a place to begin the ceremony discussion.

If you have decided to be married in either your faith or hers, you will need to find a relatively open-minded clergy person in that faith. Expect the officiant to make some adjustments to the traditional ceremonies to accommodate a marriage to the infidel. Instead of a full Catholic mass at the Cathedral, for example, you may find a priest who will perform a Cliff Notes' version of a wedding ceremony in a side chapel.

If you want to drag both religions into the gutter, you need to find two officiants who will tag team the ceremony. Depending on the combinations, this could be inspiring, annoying, or flat-out dangerous. It will almost never be easy to arrange, particularly if you are a member of any congregation that is viewed as extreme in its devotions. You might want to get started by asking your own religious leader if he or she would consider going halfsies. If this person balks, ask people who have been around a lot of weddings if they know of anyone more willing to fudge the particulars of the one true faith. Be prepared to act as intermediaries in a long and tense negotiation as you work out the details. For example, when the Voodoo priestess sacrifices the Rhode Island Red, would she be willing to allow the Rabbi to certify it as kosher? Would the schmaltz be eaten at the reception or rubbed on the newlyweds before conjugating their union?

If you and the new missus have decided to turn your backs on the religions of both of your people, you'll probably opt for a civil ceremony. If you want to bring in some of the flavor of your religious traditions, have some friends and relatives select readings for the service. Reserve veto powers for these, lest your wedding ceremony degenerate into an episode of "Crossfire."

Grilling the Officiants

You think any hack with mail-order religious credentials or a notary stamp can preside over the most important and long-lasting decision of your life? Yup. Why, someone who could participate in such a seminal event must have some sort of training, right? Nope. Truth be told, the qualifications for hitching a couple are substantially lower than for hitching a trailer. To find the divinely appointed religious leader and/or sage civic official that's right for you, you're going to have to lock the person in a windowless room, shine a light in his or her eyes and ask a few questions:

- Are there any requirements for getting married in this church/temple/mosque? Like, you wouldn't ask a fella to give up his Sunday mornings on the links, would ya? What kind of cruel God would want that?
- Are there any premarital counseling requirements? If so, will you be showing filmstrips or incorporating any other visual aids?
- Do you perform the ceremony yourself, or do you job this stuff out?
- Does the organist know "Freebird"? If not, can he or she read sheet music?
- Are there any restrictions on dress, clothing, photography, and so forth inside the sanctuary? Like, if I wanted to wear a white tux with red piping, would you be down with that?
- Are there restrictions on decorations inside the sanctuary? We were kind of thinking about a Felliniesque circus motif. Could you rubber-stamp that kind of thing, or would you have to check with HQ?
- Would your God have a problem with some of my friends and family doing some secular readings as well as biblical readings? We just wouldn't feel married if we didn't have someone read a passage from *Fear and Loathing in Las Vegas*.
- By promising to raise the kids in the faith, is that like a double-pinky swear promise or just, you know, a kind of average, everyday promise?
- OK, let's get serious. How much is this going to set me back for you, the temple, the ivory tickler, the whole enchilada?
- Do you take Discover? Are you affiliated with any of the major frequent-flyer programs?

Sacred Vows

For your sake, and the sake of all in attendance at your wedding, I really hope you'll just skip this section and do the vows by the book. Writing your own is time-consuming, politically perilous, and likely to embarrass. Chances are at least ninety-nine in one hundred that your vows are going to be icky. They will be too long, too sappy, and too obscure. On the plus side, no polite person will ever point out that they were lame, you and the wife will love them, and you might even make a fan or two among the old ladies in the crowd. Just don't allow your buddies to get liquored up before the ceremony. They're likely to heckle if you stray from the path.

Before setting pen to paper, make sure that your officiant will let this sort of sacrilege profane his or her holy temple. Some will only allow ceremonies to proceed as the one true God intended. Others need the ceremony honorarium enough to look the other way for a few minutes. If your project is green-lighted, it's time to hit the scrolls, Shakespeare.

First decide how this collaboration is going to proceed. Are you and the fiancée going to sit around and have some script meetings, or will each of you retreat to your own garret to search your soul? I would recommend the latter approach, because you actually might get something written before you start arguing. If you do go this way, you might want to get some general consensus on how the ceremony will proceed. Are you going to script the entire event, or are you only going to write short passages to read to each other at the ceremony? Also determine an appropriate length. You don't want to go off and write a snappy little "Roses are red" ditty, only to have your fiancée come back with a 107-page epic poem written in old English.

Once you have the framework, think substance first, style second. Let's face it, you don't even know what a sonnet is, so don't try to write one. (You do know what a limerick is, but there's no call for that, particularly if you are getting married in Nantucket.) Don't try to make it rhyme. Don't be afraid to be a little sappy. Don't try to show off. Keep it simple, strong, and short, short, short, short, short, and short. Oh yeah, and keep it short.

One way to start is by finding some passage that speaks to both of you. The Bible, the Bard, the great romantic poets, and Def Leppard are all reliable sources. Quote something nice and start from there. That way, you'll have a place to begin and at least part of your vows won't suck. Anything that gets that first blank page all inky usually moves the process along.

So what do you want to say? Do you each want to talk about the moment you knew this person was destined to be your mate? Do you want to talk about what love is? Do you want to explore your shared vision of the future? Would you like to discuss what it was that first attracted you to each other? The radiance of her smile, the sparkle in her eye, the jiggle in her booty? Do you wish to discuss your union in the context of your family history? Your religious beliefs? Your devotion to the Packers?

However you get there, you'll want to include two essential points:

- ◆ You really love each other.
- ◆ You commit yourselves to each other. Forever.

In fact, be sure to work in those two points and everything else will be just fine. Make your wedding vows anything you want them to be. Make your whole wedding ceremony everything you want it to be. This is the one chance you get to stand up and declare before everyone who is important to you that you and this fine babe are now one. Don't let anyone, particularly a jerk like me, tell you the best way to do that.

CHAPTER 13

The Music

Music. It stirs the soul of the savage beast. It gets Granny up dancing. It loosens brassieres in the backseat of a station wagon. Is there a more powerful force on the planet? Well, yeah. But nuclear fission is not nearly so much fun at a wedding.

As far as music goes, you're looking at two basic gigs. You will have music before, during, and after the ceremony itself. Unless you are quite the maverick, this music will be soft and pretty. You will also have music for the reception. This music should make people want to dance. Got it? Good.

Jamming on Ceremony

Oh my friends, the possibilities for mirth are so ample, right here. Glorious temptation abounds. Would it not be classic to have the organist play "We're Pink Elephants on Parade" from *Dumbo* as the bridesmaids proceed down the aisle? Wouldn't knowing this could happen actually spark an interest in the color scheme of your wedding, particularly the bridesmaids' dresses? Tell me true, Hubby, is the first song you want to hear as a married man really Pachelbel's Canon?

Alas, the ceremonial music is one place where tradition is likely to rule. Wedding ceremonies are dainty things, so the soundtrack sort of has to match. We're probably looking at relatively light orchestration here. Maybe just an organ or piano player. Maybe a few strings. Maybe a chanteuse. If you are getting married in a church or synagogue, the house ivory tickler might be appropriate. If that's not your style, you're going to have to shop around a bit. Ask the officiant if he or she has recommendations. If there's a local music school, see if it has a chamber music group that might be appropriate. You might also see if a stripped-down version of the reception band might work, maybe just a guitar or piano. This tends to be a great solution if the wedding ceremony is being held in the same place as the reception. You'll pay extra, but it should still be cheaper than booking two separate acts.

Before you set the playlist for your ceremony, be sure to check with your officiant, particularly if you are having a religious ceremony. Certain houses of worship might also place restrictions on what can be played. Some will only allow devotional music. Others would be glad to have "Sympathy for the Devil" wafting out of their stained-glass windows. While some might allow that *Footloose* song about dancing despite the church's edicts, don't play it. It sucks.

Regardless of which songs you've chosen and who fiddles them, your service will be scored in three parts. In the trade, these are referred to as "before, during, and after."

Preludes and Processionals

Before the ceremony, you should have some sort of soft, pleasant music playing as people take their seats. Usually, this music is some classically innocuous sort of thing that no one pays any attention too. This is appropriate in that the women don't need distraction as they cattily assess the shortcomings of what everyone else is wearing, and the men surreptitiously check the wedding program to see just how much they will have to sit through. This prelude music also provides a nice, dull basis of comparison for when the real action begins.

The processional is one of the great dramatic moments of your life. Close your eyes and picture this. The doors swing open. In a carefully orchestrated fashion, the wedding party advances . . . step, together; step, together. Flower petals are strewn, rings are borne, and a long white runner is rolled out as your bride appears, more dolled up than you have ever seen her or ever will again. She will take that short walk, coming to pledge herself to you, forsaking all others, for the rest of your lives. OK, now open your eyes. What was the music you just heard? If it was Mendelssohn's "Wedding March," don't be afraid to go with it, you plebian, imaginationless dolt, it's really OK. If it was that "ooga-chacka" song, I greatly applaud your vision. Go with Mendelssohn's "Wedding March." This is a wedding, for cripe's sake, not a carnival.

Ceremonial Favorites

Depending on the nature of your ceremony, the music that plays during your ceremony may be limited to religious tunes. No, "Stairway to Heaven" does not qualify as a religious tune. Nor does anything by Bob Marley, unless your religion happens to be Rastafarianism. Even if this is the case, you still might have some latitude in deciding which hymns are sung. Maybe that gospel version of "You Can't Always Get What You Want" could be worked in somehow.

If you're having a secular ceremony, or one of those watered-down religious ceremonies, you have a much larger body of potential ceremony music to draw on. This does not mean that anything goes. While that "Voulez-vous couchez avec moi" song might add a little pseudo-franco levity to the affair, it might be better saved for the reception. Go with the softies for the ceremony. Pick something nice by one of the three Bs: Bach, the Righteous or Neville Brothers, or The Beatles. If you have a friend or relative with a nice set of pipes, this might be an appropriate time to strut him or her out like a well-trained circus monkey.

The Recessional

As mentioned, this is the first tune you and your wife will ever hear as a wedded couple. Make this a good one. It should spark an air of celebration, of joy, and of a deep and profound sense of relief. How about the "Ode to Joy" from Ludwig's no. 9? How about some cool trumpet fanfare thing? How about "Whole New World," from Walt Disney's *Aladdin*? (How about closely examining where you are going with your life if you actually took that last suggestion seriously?)

Music for Party People

In theory, you could choose any kind of music you please for your reception. Let's say you and the squeeze are open-minded fans of the avant-garde. There's no law that says you can't hire an extremely large naked man to hurl cans of SpaghettiOs at a Wurlitzer while singing the entire score of *Don Giovanni* in a shrieking falsetto. Yeah, that would be . . . interesting. Or let's say you love modern jazz. That's cool, Daddio. It not only shows that your tastes are more refined than most, but it also helps cut down on all that dancing everyone seems to dislike so much. If the new ball and chain insists, you still could get out and cut the rug. Nothing gets the hips swaying like atonality.

Truth be told, the music at your reception is something that must be shared by all in attendance. It's polite to have enough variety so that everybody finds something they like at some point in the festivities. It would be even nicer if the band or DJ cranked out some dance tunes. Yes, you can have a perfectly nice reception with a quiet little string quartet playing in the corner. It will be terribly elegant. It just won't be as fun as hiring the cheesiest DJ ever to hang a disco ball.

Oh yeah, no matter who you hire to provide the music for your reception, make sure that "your song" gets played. If you and your fiancée don't have a song, get one. Every couple needs a song.

Spinner or Strummer

This leads us to the defining decision you need to make about your reception music. Are you going with a band or a DJ? There are diehard advocates for both approaches, and you can make a case either way. Most folks these days wind up with a DJ. It's kind of hard to argue with that from a practical basis.

Undoubtedly, a good DJ will cost a lot less than even a bad band. DJs are also a lot more predictable than bands because even a bad one will have a pretty decent music collection. You don't have to sit down and spec out every song that gets played, but you can offer a list of songs you want. More important, you can ban the songs you don't want. Of course, since the songs are all recorded, you'll have few concerns about what the song will sound like. About the only way a DJ can screw up the music is to drop the needle in the wrong place.

Unfortunately, this doesn't mean that the DJ is not capable of screwing up the entire evening. Most wedding DJs suffer from the misguided impression that you want to hear them speak. Virtually nothing is more pathetically annoying than the continual party-festive haranguing of a bad wedding DJ. In some cases, people's eyes have rolled so far back in their heads that their irises were never ever seen again.

The solution here is simple. Steal his microphone. Or at the very least, promise him great bodily harm if he ever threatens to use it again. In some cases, you might actually have to script out what the DJ may and may not say. For example, as you enter the reception hall he may introduce you and your bride as the new Mr. and Mrs. Blaufeld (given, of course, your name is Blaufeld and he knows how to pronounce it correctly). He may, at no time, say anything like, "C'mon Grandma, shake your groove thing!"

To head off the worst-case scenario, you should take a look at your DJ in action before you sign him on. This isn't quite so critical as it will be with a band, but still a good idea. If you are satisfied that he's only kind of a jerk, book him early. Just make sure he knows the time, date, location, and dress code. And make sure you understand how much he will cost and how long he will spin platters.

Playing with the Band

Having a live band for your wedding reception is way better than a DJ, except for those frequent occasions when it is way worse. In other words, there is a lot more room for variation here. Believe me, you really want to do your homework when hiring a band.

The first call you'll want to make is what general style of music you want. Some of this is about musical taste. More of it is about money. Would a full-up, jumping-at-the-Savoy swing band be great at your wedding? Invariably. It's just going to cost you vast multiples of what a nice little four- or five-member wedding band will. This may be worth it to you. It may not be.

You also want to take into consideration the ethnic backgrounds of your guests. I'll tell you right here, if you come from a big Polish family, you would not be well advised to hire a samba band. Polkas just don't sound the same when played on the marimbas.

Likewise, a couple guys in lederhosen just ain't gonna be a big hit at a Jewish wedding. "Hava Nagila" just don't cut it as an oompah song.

Finally, think about what we will call the wedding-ality of your band. There may be a great local club band you've seen a few times. They play most of their own tunes and play them well. You've never had anything but fun at one of their gigs. Good choice? Probably not. You see, this band likely suffers from a malady known in select circles as "musical integrity." They probably just care a little too darn much about what kind of noise comes out of their speakers. This can cause a major problem. When asked if they would mind playing "Daddy's Little Girl" when your wife dances with her father, they might refuse. This would not be a bad thing, except for the fact that your father-in-law likes the song and he's paying for the wedding.

Clearly, the safer choice is to hire a bunch of broken-spirited never-beens who have cobbled themselves into a wedding band in a marginal attempt to cover the mortgages on their trailers. These sad troubadours may once have had ambitions of stardom, but years of pumping out "The Bride Cuts the Cake" to the tune of "The Farmer in the Dell" has bled them of all their essential life juices. Now, supported by cheap hooch and spandex, they will take any request you throw at them without a break in their pasted-on smiles. Like long broken horses, they will jump over any hedgerow you choose. These guys really know how to light up a party!

Regardless of which direction you want to go in, don't hire a band until you've seen them play. If you can see them a few times, all the better. If you like what you see, go ahead and nail down the details. Get the following down in writing:

- The date, time, and exact location of the reception
- Their arrival time
- The length of time they will play
- The cost and what, if anything, incurs extra charges
- The names of all the band members (You want to know if they're switching anyone out on you.)

Finally, once you've decided on a band or a DJ, make sure they contact the reception hall to discuss any technical issues. They should know where they are setting up, whether the hall is wired for their equipment, if they will need to bring in any lighting, and any other logistical concerns. The last thing you want is for the band to spend half the evening looking for places to plug in.

Recommended Musical Selections

	Songs to Consider if You Can Get Away with It	Songs to Prevent Your Bride from Even Considering	Songs You Will Have to Choose to Keep Peace in the Family
Processional	"Feets Don't Fail Me Now"	"These Boots Were Made for Walking"	"Here Comes the Bride"
Recessional	"I Wanna Be Sedated"	"Tomorrow Belongs to Me"	Pachelbel's Canon
Bride and Groom First Dance	"Having My Baby"	"Man Smart (Woman Smarter)"	"Unchained Melody"
Bride and Father Dance	"Papa's Got a Brand New Bag"	"Daddy's Little Girl"	"Daddy's Little Girl"
Groom and Mother Dance	"Mammie"	"Mother's Little Helper"	"Sunrise, Sunset"

CHAPTER 14

The Photographer

You've been to Sears. You've seen those signs advertising the family portrait package. What was that deal? Something like $29.99 for an 8 × 10, a few 5 × 7s, and a sheet of wallet-size snaps. It's really a heck of a package. You have your choice of maybe twenty different backgrounds, including Mad King Ludwig's castle and the Malibu coastline. Correct me if I'm wrong, but you might even get a free photo refrigerator magnet if you play your cards right.

Being a man of reason, you understand that the photo documentation of your nuptials and ensuing revelry is likely to be a tad pricier than the Alpine meadow in Sears. You know your photographer has to truck out there and take a bunch more pictures. The printing might also be a bit more, and you will almost definitely need some extra refrigerator magnets for the 'rents and bridal party. Let's be bold here. Let's say it will cost more than ten times more than Sears finest.

Twenty?

Thirty?

Nice try, but here's the ugly truth. For what you will end up paying for some snaps of your wedding, you could march right past the Sears shutterbug, head straight down to the Craftsman section, and snap up that big honking mechanics set you've coveted since you built your first go-cart. You know, the one with 1,246 pieces and a tall stack of big red tool cabinets. Then you could wander over and buy a forty-gallon, five-horsepower compressor with a rather robust set of air tools. And just for good measure why don't you toss in a smattering of those miracle tools Bob Vila peddles on late night TV? But try not to think about all that when your wedding photographer takes your picture. It may be hard to smile.

That's not even the worst of it. What's really going to kill you is that you're going to shell out thousands of dollars for a professional photographer, and the best picture of your wedding will come out of some little pocket-sized disposable camera your Aunt Trudy bought at KMart. This is not because Aunt Trudy is such a talented photographer. It's because a hundred people are going to take an average of 36 pictures each. Of those 3,600 pictures, 3,596 will suck. Three will be kind of fun. One will be great.

Unfortunately, this does not make the wedding photographer a highly dispensable line item. I'm guessing that you and your better half will want a nice wedding portrait for the mantle and a well-constructed photo album you can take down and look at every eight to ten years or so. All of the key players in your wedding will also want a nice portrait of themselves and the happy couple. That means you will probably need about six to ten different pictures of reasonably good quality. Taking good pictures on a consistent basis is not that easy. If you want someone to get a good shot of all the combinations and permutations of family and friends you need covered, you'll have to hire a pro. If you choose anyone other than the blatantly wrong photographer, you will get at least an acceptable shot of everyone who needs to be photographed at the wedding.

Picking the Pro

What makes the difference between a good photographer and a bad photographer? You have to look at three sets of factors. The least important is the quality of the pictures he or she takes. The second most important is the general tumult he or she creates while taking those pictures. The most important is the relative lack of honor, honesty, and just plain decency the photographer will exhibit in the course of your business dealings. Let's start there.

Not all wedding photographers are con artists. I personally know of at least one who would not be better suited running a rigged ring-toss game at a traveling carny. There are, however, more than a few bad seeds. I heartily recommend that you check a photographer's references, and Better Business Bureau rap sheet, before you even look at his or her portfolio. Even better, use a photographer who has done satisfactory work for someone you know. These people need to be checked out carefully. After all, what good are great pictures you will never see?

Checking references will also give you a sense of what this guy is like to be around. Is he prompt, professional, and courteous? Does she deliver the prints on schedule? Does he show up drunk and ask the bridesmaids if they want to do a little after-hours photo session in a suite upstairs? (Would he share those pictures with the groom in the unlikely event that one or more of them said yes?)

When you ask for references, make sure you don't just get two people who will shill for him or her. Ask for at least three references within the last six months. When you call, ask them if you could see some pictures from their wedding. Maybe they could invite you over for dinner. It wouldn't have to be fancy. You wouldn't want them to go out of their way or anything.

Once you've found a few shutter bugs who are neither cretins nor crooks, you may want to see if he or she knows which end of the camera to point at the subjects. This can be accomplished by looking at pictures already taken. Are they thoughtfully composed and elegantly lit? Are the colors rich and saturated? Do the bride's eyes glow red like the demon spawn? If you are not comfortable assessing whether you think a picture is good or bad, bring along someone who is an avid amateur photographer. His or her opinion will be no more or less valid than yours, but it should be fun watching the pro be peppered with a flurry of annoying and irrelevant questions.

This initial screening should also give you a sense of how well you get along with this person. This is important. You will be spending a good portion of a big day with him or her. If the photographer really gets on your nerves for some reason, it's just not worth it. It will just end up putting you in a sour mood for your reception.

Now that you've culled the heard, here are a few questions you'll want to hit the survivors with:

- Will your camera suck my immortal soul through the lens? Have you had your equipment checked for that? (Can't be too careful, right?)
- How long have you been in business?
- How many fraud indictments have you collected in that period?
- Do you do this full time, or are you some frustrated accountant who gets his ya-yas out by shooting chicks in big white dresses?
- Can we buy the negatives? How much will they cost? If not, how long will you keep them?
- Where will you be doing the formal portraits? Will you use more than one background?
- How many shots can we expect to see? What about portrait setups and general kinds of candids?
- How long will you stay and shoot candids?

- Will you add our suggestions to your shot list?
- Will you shoot both color and black and white?
- If we say "jump," will you say "how high?" (If he or she says "yes," hire someone else. This one's a liar.)

You will also want to make sure that you really nail down your photographer on price. A lot of studios have a very reasonable-sounding base package. By the time you drive it off the lot, however, you can double or triple the price on extras. Make sure you understand everything that is considered over and above the package price and that you get all of that in writing. Your contract should also include the date and time of your wedding and the name of the photographer who will cover the event. (Some studios employ dozens. You want to know who you're getting.) Ask these questions:

- How much does the base package cost, and exactly what does it include?
- What other packages are offered?
- In addition to the package fee, are there any hourly fees, travel costs, or other standard charges?
- How much will it cost for additional prints outside the package?
- What if I want to order more prints in the future? Will those costs be guaranteed?

Cropping Costs

Once you've decided who will be scurrying about annoying everyone at your wedding, you should have a little tête-à-tête to map out the battle plan. This is when he or she will find out everything you would like covered, and you will find out you can't afford it. There's likely to be a little give and take in this process. For example, you'll give the photographer a lot of money. And he or she will take it.

Actually, if the costs are getting too high, there are a few ways to bring them back under control. In a lot of these scenarios, the printing is actually a lot more expensive than the shooting. If you can keep the number of prints down, you can save a lot of money. Consider sending pictures only to those people who really want them. Your parents and grandparents will probably qualify. Your bridesmaids may. Your ushers won't.

Another way to get the cost down is to have the pro cover only part of the wedding and rely on the amateurs to fill in the gaps. For example, you could have the wedding photographer cover the ceremony and the formal portraits, then have family and friends shoot lots of pictures of each other at the reception. If you just want to make sure you have a nice picture for the mantle, this can save some serious jack. If getting exactly the right shot of you cutting a cake is important to you, keep the pro for the whole gig. I would suggest, however, that the pro be dismissed before you head back to the hotel for your wedding night. You don't want those shots winding up on the Internet.

If you are limiting the amount of professional coverage, do what you can to increase the amateur photography. Buy a whole batch of decent disposable cameras and put them on all the tables. Ask a few friends to bring cameras. You may be surprised at how many good shots you'll get and at how unattractive most of your friends and family really are. Yowza!

Timing Is Everything

The superstitious may feel that it is bad luck for the groom to see the bride before the wedding. They may also feel that it is sound practice to grab a black cat by the tail and swing it over their head three times to ward off the bad voodoo. Both of these practices are dumb. There are a pile of good reasons to get your formal portraits over with before your wedding ceremony.

First, you will get better pictures. Good portraits take a lot of time to properly light and frame. If your photographer doesn't have to worry about getting you back to the reception quickly, he or she can be a bit more methodical about it.

Second, you may have better choices for where you want your portraits taken. Instead of the church or reception site, you may prefer a local park, beach, or scenic overlook. If you shoot your portraits earlier, you can travel a bit farther for the right location than you might want to after the ceremony.

Third, you're likely to be all fidgety on your wedding day, waiting around for the ceremony to get going. This will give you something to do.

Most important, you might actually want to attend your own reception. The food is good. The bar is open. And there are tons of people you haven't seen for a long time. Why spend the whole time smiling into a camera when you could be having fun? Once you get through that ceremony part, you're probably going to be ready to party a bit. Unless waiting around for a fat, little bald guy to adjust his f-stop is your idea of a party, the portrait thing will come as a bit of a buzz kill.

Ignore all this sage advice at your own peril. You will end up pissed at your photographer for taking too long. Your bar bill will skyrocket as your guests get all tanked up waiting for the new Mr. and Mrs. to make their entrance. And you will work twice as hard getting around to see everyone at dinner because you've had no chance to knock off a few at the reception. If you just can't get over the superstition part, do what any rational person would do in the early part of the twenty-first century. Grab a black cat by the tail and swing it over your head three times.

CHAPTER 15

The Videographer

This is what you should know about videographers: You don't need one. You don't want one. If anyone suggests that you may need and/or want one, you should run away screaming in terror as if you were being chased by ghouls from *The Night of the Living Dead*. And I'm not talking about those wussy little stumble-behind-the-car ghouls in the beginning of the movie. I'm talking punch-through-the-door-and-munch-a-starlet ghouls.

With rare exceptions, wedding videographers are miserable little cretins with no legitimate place in a civilized society. (If you happen to be a videographer, I apologize. It's probably not your fault that you're a miserable little cretin.) When dealing with one of these guys, always remember that you are talking to someone who is trying to turn something he hates (being a wedding videographer) into something he loves (being a movie director).

If you elect to display the severe misjudgment of hiring one of these creatures, he[1] will seek revenge for his failed existence on you, your spouse, your families, and your friends. He will hunt you down like a rabid coyote, turn his ugly klieg light upon you, and make you perform like a trained seal at a traveling circus. All of this will be for the benefit of a tape that 99 percent of us will never see more than once.

That other 1 percent? They're the lucky devils who paid handsomely to be shamed and degraded at regular intervals as their least-favorite, wedding-crazed in-laws inflict their wedding video upon unwitting guests at every family gathering until death do they part. If you become one of these unfortunate souls, death cannot you part fast enough.

At most weddings where a videographer is present, there is actually one moment at which he enlivens the festivities. This moment comes when one of your more aggressive, and perhaps inebriated, guests finally gives into the temptation to take a swing at the little creep. This is one of the few moments of your wedding that you will truly want to capture on tape. Your videographer is almost certain to miss the shot.

So you're going to do it anyhow? Fine, be that way. But don't come crying to me, Wedding Boy. I told you so. I told you so. I told you so. I told you so.

---

1. I use the male gender when speaking of videographers because the proportion of men to women in the profession is about the same as that of a typical high school AV club: nine guys who can't get laid for every one girl who won't go out with them.

What You Should Look for in a Videographer

Let's start with the basics. When interviewing a videographer, think personality first, professional qualities second. This will make it marginally less likely that you will trade a far less pleasant wedding for a slightly better videotape of the event. Is this man of sound mind and good character? Does he bathe at least occasionally? Does he wear a monocle? Is he bald? Will he shave his head and wear a monocle if you pay him an extra fifty bucks?

Most important, does the little creep (they are almost always little) understand that your wedding is not being staged for his benefit? This one question will narrow the field considerably. In fact, it will narrow it to maybe one guy in Jersey and another in Sri Lanka. Since you are not likely to be hiring either of these guys, you are going to have to lay down the law. I suggest you do this with great conviction:

Start by saying, "I want you to be inconspicuous. In fact, I don't want to know you are there."

He's thinking, "Well, I suppose we won't have to run tracks down the aisle for the dolly moves, but the boom is a must, the ladder shot stays, and I'll need at least four hours with my principals for close-ups." He says, "I'm the invisible man. Did you see that picture? It's a very important film."

You grab a fistful of shirt and repeat, with conviction, "I don't want to know you are there."

He thinks, "Talent can be sooooooooooooooooo temperamental. You have to treat them like children." He nods.

You lower your voice to an icy, freakish snarl and mutter, "I have a large collection of medieval torture equipment, and I'm looking for an opportunity to use it."

He thinks, "*Braveheart* was a good film, but it had flaws. The butch thing is just so done, and Mel . . . he's fabulous, but he was all wrong for the project." He says, "I see."

You say, "If you ruin my wedding, I will hurt you."

He thinks, "If he ruins my film, he'll never get married in this town again."

If You Want to Get Technical About This . . .

Now that you've laid down the law, you might actually want to see if this guy knows how to work his camera. Ask him to show you some samples of his work. With the current state of professional equipment, you should be looking at something that at least approaches the video and audio quality of the evening news. The picture should be consistently clear. The colors should be bright, and the lighting should be relatively even. If people disappear when they are in the shadows or are backlit, you have a problem. Just as important, the sound should be consistently audible and balanced.

Videos that look too slick should also raise a red flag. Hollywood-style production values can't be grabbed on the fly. If the video is perfectly lit, the shots ideally framed, and the sound invariably pristine, you know that the couple made unusually large accommodations for the video crew. Some people are just like that. I suspect you are not one of them, as most of their kind would have stopped reading somewhere back around that "miserable little cretin" crack.

To get a sense of your videographer's level of professionalism, ask what kind of equipment he uses. The likely formats are Beta or some form of digital video. Higher-end outfits may shoot on digi-beta. All of these formats are acceptable. Cheaper guys may use hi-8, 8mm, or VHS. These are a pretty clear-cut indication that you are dealing with an amateur. You may also want to ask what kind of editing system he uses. Final Cut Pro is the most likely standard, but higher-end places will use either Media 100 or Avid systems. All of these systems are perfectly adequate tools for the job if your editor knows what buttons to push.

Since the guy who shoots your video will also probably edit it, you will want to take a close look at how well he can tell a story.

Did he capture the key moments? Does the video seem to progress in a logical manner? Are the transitions from one scene to the next smooth? Do you like the way he uses background music? Does it look like the sample reel from Cheeseball Special Effect Corp? Most important, can he keep up the pace? Wedding videos tend to move slower than a Yugo pulling a horse trailer. You should also ask to see a work in progress just to make sure there's no bait and switch going on.

If you are still awake after seeing the samples, it's time to talk about his approach. Does he go in solo with one camera, or does he bring in a crew with multiple setups? You will get a better final video with a few cameras, but you will pay a price. It's not only more expensive to have all the extra assistants, but you will have three times the cretins running around the joint. Think long and hard about this. You can always send your groomsman to tune up the videographer when things get ugly. If he's got a crew watching his back, the situation could get out of control.

Speaking about getting out of control, you should make sure that your videographer and photographer speak with each other well in advance of the wedding. If you have a full video crew and a photographer all going after the same shot, it can get pretty crowded. If they can't come to an agreement on their own, you'll have to set up some guidelines. Personally, I would recommend some sort of pro-wrestling-style contest to determine who gets dibs on the best angles. If they won't go for that, dueling pistols, foils, or sabers would all do just fine. Just remember one thing: Your wedding picture will sit on a prominent shelf in your home, where you will see it every day for the rest of your life. Your wedding video will also sit on a shelf in your home for the rest of your life.

Of course, you should get references and check them carefully before signing anything other than do-not-resuscitate orders for your videographer. Ask him to list out exactly what they are providing for what they are delivering. Some charge by the hour and others by the project. If your guy charges by the hour, find out what happens if he goes over his estimated hours. You should also check how much it costs for extra copies. It's always a good idea to have several made in case something happens to the original. That way, you can be secure in the knowledge that you will always have a copy of the one tape you will never watch again.

The Cheese Platter

Now that you've got your man, you'll want to discuss the basic style of the video. Your basic approaches include cheesy, extra-cheesy, and just-hit-me-with-a-mallet.

The simplest approach involves a single camera, edited simply. More often than not, the video guy will throw in a few gauzy filters and odd sparkly effects for no apparent reason. Still, this is likely to be the cheapest and least intrusive option.

Next stop down the *fromage* aisle is the "documentary." It follows you through your wedding day as you, your bride, and the rest of the wedding party get ready for the big event. Of course, it continues through the wedding and the reception, cutting away to interviews with those who know you best. This all sounds well and good, until you really think it through. Now you don't just have a failed auteur popping up behind the priest at your ceremony. Both of you have one attached to your side for an entire day. This will be vaguely reminiscent of that leech scene in *The African Queen*. This brand of torture also costs a lot more money.

Looking for more cheese than a Wisconsin smorgasbord? Try the nostalgic approach. We begin with a delightful still montage of you and your bride as babies. We see snippets of home video as you two cute little devils mature. But, hark, what's this? Is that video of you two lovebirds dancing together at your cousin Johnny's wedding? And doesn't that double-heart special effect make it all the more special? The nostalgic approach proceeds through the day in similar style, yanking every soft-focus special effect out of the drawer. This is also the oeuvre that is most likely to send someone out to harass every guest at every table into wishing virtually identical best wishes. Believe me, this will only be amusing if your family and friends are unusually heavy drinkers.

Depending on which approach you are bludgeoned into accepting, the cost for these little treats is likely to run from about $500 for a rank amateur with the camera he got for his bar mitzvah, to well over $1,500 for an experienced huckster with several accomplices. In other terms, you pay the equivalent of renting up to five hundred quality videos you actually may want to see someday. In fact, that might just be the solution. Skip the wedding video and go rent *Father of the Bride*, *The Wedding Singer*, and *Seven Brides for Seven Brothers*. The result will be less stressful, infinitely more entertaining, and a whole lot cheaper.

CHAPTER 16

The Dress Code

There are those among us with an innate sense of style. You've met these guys. Never wrinkled. Always in well-fitting suits and well-shined shoes, as if everything they own came right out of the box. Sure, most of these guys are gay, but not all of them. A whole bunch are just European or something. In any case, I'm not talking to these guys. They already have a tuxedo and it fits perfectly.

This chapter is for us all-American guys. Guys with hard-won stains on their clothes. Guys who may own an iron but couldn't tell you how to use it or even where it is. We are the men who prop up the great American T-shirt industry. "Who's with stupid?" We're with stupid. Except when our shirts offer "Hot Babe Breathalyzer Test. Put your lips here and blow." (Dang, how do these comic geniuses keep coming up with this stuff?)

Can we count you among our ranks? Take this simple test:

1. I wear something with a team logo:
   (a) whenever I'm either awake or asleep.
   (b) once a day.
   (c) in the shower.
   (d) ooooh that's so camp. Don't you just love it?
2. Sweatpants:
   (a) are what I will be buried in.
   (b) need replacing once a decade or so.
   (c) can go months without washing.
   (d) make my hips look big.
3. My T-shirt collection:
   (a) takes more than one drawer of my dresser.
   (b) contains at least one amusingly sexist slogan.
   (c) proudly reflects my tastes in music.
   (d) is all from Banana Republic.
4. My pajamas:
   (a) are boxer shorts.
   (b) are sweatpants.
   (c) are nonexistent.
   (d) are silk.

If you answered anything but "d" to any of the above, read on. It's going to take more than a bit of work to get you to the church on time. For you "d" guys, we'll see you next time we're in Europe.

The Penguin Suit

Let's make this simple. There are two things you could wear to your wedding: a tuxedo or not a tuxedo. Since most of us already know everything about the not-a-tuxedo option let's skip that one. As for the penguin suit, here's what you need to know: strap it on and look in the mirror. If you can convincingly say, "Bond. James Bond," it's a good tuxedo. If you can more convincingly say, "On this, the day of my bar mitzvah . . . ," it's a bad tuxedo.

If you're going by the book, the appropriate choice of formal wear depends on the season, the time of day, and the relative formality of your wedding. A proper gent might wear a tailcoat, a dinner jacket, an ascot, a cutaway, or a stroller. Many of these styles can be appropriately worn in a variety of colors with an assortment of accessories. You, my friend, will not be given these choices. The fashion trigonometry is so complex that it must remain the exclusive domain of homosexuals and Europeans. For a stylistically challenged guy like you, we're going to keep the choices simple.

You will wear a traditional tuxedo, and it will be black. You may choose whether you want a shawl collar, a notch collar, or a peak collar. Boom. Done.

Your shirt will be white. It may be plain front or pleated, but will not have ruffles. You may choose a wing or turndown collar. Boom. Done.

You will wear a bow tie, which you will learn to tie yourself. It should be black. It can be in a simple color to match your cummerbund or vest, but it shouldn't be. You can't be trusted to choose a simple color. Boom. Done.

You can wear a simple cummerbund or a simple vest. Black would be best, but a simple color is acceptable. Boom. Done.

Your shoes will be black and shiny. If you want to spring for patent leather shoes, go right ahead. If not, highly polished calf dress shoes will suffice. Wear black socks. Boom. Done.

Wear shirt studs and cuff links. Add a wedding band before the night is over. Boom. Done.

Are there more options than all of the above? Absolutely. Will I tell you what they are? No way. If you don't already know what they are, you can't handle them. I also will not try to tell you what's in style this year. You should never ask. The classic black tux with simple accessories is always in style. Some of the alternates that are occasionally in vogue are invariably embarrassing just a few years later. Don't believe me? Ask any of those guys who wore a powder blue, velvet tux over a wide-lapel puffy shirt in the 1970s. How many of those guys don't wince every time they look at their wedding portrait on the mantle? If some guy at the tux store tells you that the man-skirt is all the rage in this year's formal wear, run, do not walk, out the door. Otherwise you will live to rue the day you met him.

Fit and Trim

Now that you know what to ask for, you'll have to decide where to get it. Your first choice will be whether you want to buy it or rent it. You'll decide to buy it. Part of that decision will be based on the fact that rentals cost more than a third as much as just buying the thing, so you might as well go ahead and snap it up. Part of that decision will be based on the fact that if you buy one, it can be tailored to fit you. Most of that decision will be based on the knowledge that almost all tuxedo rentals are for proms and weddings. All those guys who wore that suit before you, what do you suppose they were doing on their prom and wedding nights?

If you are kinky enough to like that idea, make sure you pick up your rental pants and jacket early enough to discover that they don't fit really well. Make double sure you return the tux on time. Those places totally stick you on per-day charges if you space and bring it back after your honeymoon.

If you are buying a tux, you might want to shop around a bit. Try some of the local department stores and menswear shops as well as the men's formal wear store at the mall. You're going to find a very wide range of prices here. These will mostly be driven by the quality of the material, the workmanship, and the label. A good tux is basically just a good suit and should cost about the same. The cheap ones are all shiny and the pieces don't quite fit the way they should. The very expensive ones are mostly charging you for the label. Most of us would do well to stick in the middle range.

The one place you don't want to skimp is on the alterations. The tuxedo will not properly fit until it's altered to your measurements.

Buy one at a place that has a competent tailor, or bring it to your local tailor. If it fits properly, the lines should be smooth and clean, and it won't feel like a straitjacket. The pants should just touch the tops of your shoes and should fit comfortably around your waist.

Make sure your shirt fits equally well. Most guys wear their shirts at least one size too small, cutting off circulation to the brain. This is not only uncomfortable, but might just explain why we find those T-shirt collections of ours so amusing.

CHAPTER 17

The Ride

For some inexplicable reason, it has been decreed that those getting married must not operate motor vehicles between the end of the ceremony and the beginning of the reception. It has been further decreed that a bride must not arrive at the wedding in a conveyance that is less that thirty feet in length. This means you will probably be renting a big, white prom limo for your wedding, even if the church is next door to her house and the reception is three blocks down the road.

Sorry, that's the law.

Of course, with the proper legal representation, you might just be able to squeeze through a loophole in the wedding transportation act. This states that you will be allowed to forgo the limousine if you rent something that is even more ridiculous than a thirty-five-foot Lincoln Town Car. Some of the most popular choices are:

- ◆ **A horse-drawn carriage:** Not altogether ridiculous unless you string together eight or nine horses and get a really big carriage. Yeah, you'll think you look just like the royal family, but you'll actually end up looking like the Budweiser beer wagon.
- ◆ **A rickshaw:** Nothing says wedding-day-party-festive like a really sweaty guy re-creating the charming colonial past.
- ◆ **A hot-air balloon:** This makes quite the dramatic entrance, particularly if a little gust causes you to overshoot the churchyard and wind up in the excrement-holding ponds of the neighboring swine farm.
- ◆ **A gondola:** Now we're cooking with gas. It's classy. It's goony. It comes with its own set of tunes. The only drawback is that gondolas are really slow, particularly if your wedding is nowhere near the water.

Are there other cool ways to get to the church on time? Of course. Use your imagination. As long as they are laughably ridiculous and expensive to rent, you are free to use any conveyance you choose. With that sort of selection available, you would think that a lot more of us would be flying around town in jetpacks. Truth be told, almost everyone rents the plain-old, workaday limo. So much for American ingenuity.

Every Car Needs a Bar

In the entire span of your life, there will be only three days when it is other than ridiculous to ride around town in an immensely large, white stretch Cadillac. Your prom, your wedding, and the night you are nominated for an Academy Award. If you don't expect to be fondling Oscar anytime in the near future, sit back and enjoy the ride, Wedding Boy, because you sure ain't going to any more proms.

Unlike most things in life, limousines can be too big. It's semi-silly to be seen in a regular-size stretch. Only Yosemite Sam can get away with riding around town in a super-stretch. This goes double for any car that did not start out life as a Caddy, a Lincoln, or a Benz. Can you rent a forty-foot-long Corvette for the occasion? Probably. But you might as well get married in huge red shoes, polka-dotted balloon pants, and a foam nose. It would make you appear slightly less ridiculous. And a stretch SUV . . . it's not a limo. It's an airport bus.

One option you might want to consider is renting a classic car for the occasion. A lot of limo-rental companies have an old Rolls or Bentley on the lot, and a few specialize in exotic antiques. It's not that these are less silly than their modern-day counterparts; they're just a more fun kind of silly. It sort of works like this. Let's say your limo driver's name is Bob. If he's driving a stretch Caddy, you'll say something like, "Let's go, Bob." If he's driving a vintage Rolls, you'll say something like, "Take us through the park, Robert. You know how much I love the park." Just be sure to tip Bob really well. He'll deserve it.

Sizing up the Limousines

Renting a limo for the day is a pretty simple procedure. You really could just call up, tell them what kind of car you want and how long you want it for, and you're done. Of course, that would be just a little too simple for a wedding thing. What you're going to want to do is go down to the limousine company yourself, ask a series of prying questions, inspect all their cars, and check an extensive series of references.

It's actually a good idea to go check out the car you'll be using on your big day. The inside of limos range from ultra-swank to ultra-funky. Remember, much like those rental tuxes, the other big market for big, white limos is proms. Remember what you did on your prom night? In any case, you should check around and make sure this company has a rep for delivering clean cars on time. Make sure you also get a written list of all the extras you asked them to supply and what they will cost you. If you want them to have a TV, a cold bottle of champagne, and vast collection of Mott the Hoople CDs, make sure they supply the specific costs of each extra. It's also generally a good idea to make sure the limo company is properly licensed and insured.

Order the limo for a half hour or so before you need it. It's worth a few bucks not to worry if they are a few minutes late. You may want to have the limo wait through the ceremony and go home after they deliver you to the reception. If you want them to hang until the reception is over, you'll end up paying a lot of waiting time. You might do better sending the first one home and ordering a second limo to pick you up at the reception. In either case, keeping a car for the getaway might be a good idea. Think about it—everyone seems to get driven to the ceremony before they've had anything to drink and to the reception after they've maybe had a sip of wine. They go to the reception where the open bar lasts for five hours, and then they drive away themselves. I wouldn't recommend it. Driving your getaway car into a busload of crippled orphans can be a serious downer on your wedding night.

If you really want to get swank, you can order a whole herd of wild limousines to take the entire bridal party from the ceremony to the reception. While this does add a few shekels to the tally, it can be an awful lot of fun. Unfortunately, most limo drivers cannot be talked into match-racing their steeds, even if you promise to tip heavily. If you go this route, make sure everyone knows which car they go in, and the drivers know how many passengers they're supposed to have. You don't want to inadvertently leave Grandma sleeping in her pew.

Tin Cans and Streamers

If your friends are worth anything at all, they will completely trash the car you will be using to drive away from the wedding. If they are nice friends, they'll just tie some cans to the bumper, paint a couple of borderline-vulgar wedding night wishes in shaving cream, and leave it at that. If they are not nice, they will have taken your ride down to the chop shop and had it converted into a rolling champagne-glass love tub. If you know your friends are of the not-nice variety, you may want to take the necessary precautions. Tell one of them that your car is in the shop, and plead with him to borrow his. Then see if the little buggers are so quick to hide dead fish in the trunk.

No matter what the cretins did to the car, make sure you can see out of the windows before you drive off. Technically, those tiny little stickers with your college logo may not be legally placed in the back window of your vehicle. A totally soaped rear windshield with a slogan that reads "Warning: Newlyweds Coming" may be considered by some law enforcement officers to be even more of an obstruction. Yes, a cop would have to be a real prick to give you a ticket for driving a decorated wedding car. Yes, some cops are real pricks.

CHAPTER 18

Cash and Prizes

N ow we're getting to the good part. In case no one has clued you in, you can expect to get a couple of presents for your wedding. And we're not talking teeny-weeny, little stocking stuffers here. We're talking boatloads of big, honking, under-the-tree presents. You and your intended are going to get engagement presents, shower presents, and bachelor/bachelorette party presents. And the biggest presents of all the presents you're ever going to get . . . wedding presents.

One of the coolest parts about wedding presents is that you get to tell everyone exactly what you want them to buy you and where you want them to buy it. On paper this is the best thing you've had going since you stopped mailing letters to the North Pole. It's a lot like winning one of those one-millionth shopper contests where you get two minutes to run around the department store frantically stuffing everything in a shopping cart. There's just one little catch. If you push your cart outside the housewares section, the wheels fall off.

You see, a very cruel irony lurks at the heart of the wedding-present game. On the one hand, presents show up like you have a premium set of Polaroids of Santa in a compromising position. On the other hand, almost all of those presents are things you can cook in, eat off of, or sleep on. I understand that some guys are down with this. If you're the kind of man who stays up late watching reruns of "Emeril Live" on the Food Network, you are in for one hell of a party. Mr. Doughboy, you are about to get your puffy little hands on a veritable cornucopia of cappuccino machines, roasting pans, stemware, and table linens. You are forgiven for being all atwitter.

On the other hand, if you're the kind of guy who watches the tube while the new missus plays in the kitchen, you may be in for a little bit of disappointment here. In the mounting Mount Kilimanjaro of boxes flooding into your home like relief aid to Africa, you will find absolutely none of the following:

- Fishing tackle
- Stereo components
- Bird dogs
- Speedboats
- Beer
- Golf equipment
- Surf and/or boogie boards
- Power tools
- Fun things
- Things you actually want

Instead, here's a list of what you will find:

- Things you don't like
- Things you like well enough, but don't really care about

Here's what's at the heart of the problem: The central assumption behind the whole wedding-present thing is that the happy young couple is now leaving their parents' homes for the first time and setting up shop together. Therefore, it makes sense for their clans to supply them with all the household goods they'll need. If you are fortunate enough to be in this position, consider yourself ahead of the game. At least all those wedding presents will be useful. Not fun, but useful.

For many of you, however, both man and wife have lived on their own for a while before deciding to get hitched. You already have two toasters, two sets of dishes, two frying pans, and two coffeemakers. What you don't have is a really cool HDTV-equipped Plasma screen TV and a set of titanium wedges. So what are you going to do? You're going to march right down to the nearest department store and register for a third toaster, fry pan, coffeemaker, and set of dishes.

You will do this because people will tell you that you want china and crystal for your wedding because this is stuff "You wouldn't buy for yourself." Instead of seeing this as a gigantic neon sign of utter indifference, they will assume your lack of interest in spending thousands of dollars on plates has been a painstaking act of Spartan denial. Of course you want a soup tureen. You want it bad. You've just managed to hold yourself back until this very moment so that you could participate in this great prenuptial tableware orgy.

Yeah, go ahead and laugh about this if you can. Unfortunately, your fiancée will see the flawless logic in this. The most independent and accomplished women on the planet can somehow get all "Ozzie and Harriet" as the wedding approaches. She may have no interest in learning how to boil water, yet she will still somehow envision the day she appears from the kitchen with silver platters of Thanksgiving delights, every bit the perfect hostess. Overcome by this vision of herself as a sort of younger Martha Stewart, she will still insist that you register for $800 Calphalon anodized aluminum sauciers, casseroles, and omelette pans. In extreme cases, she'll even spend the cash you set aside for fairway woods and use it to round out the cookware set.

Goodbye Callaway. Hello Calphalon.

Registered Insanity

If left to their own devices, at least some of your friends might actually get you something you want as a wedding present. To make sure this doesn't happen, the women of the world got together at their secret headquarters and invented the bridal registry. (I don't know the precise location of this coven, but I'm thinking that you probably have to enter it through a shoe store.)

Bridal registries are a pretty simple piece of business. You go to the registry office at the store of "your" choice and say you want to register. They will give you a list of about 861,486 things you don't really care about, and you and your fiancée will spend the next three weekends inspecting each and every one of them. If you go to a high-end place, the two of you will be joined by a well-coifed, old lady who will continually encourage you to register for more expensive stuff. Through this exhaustive process, "you" will decide on the blender of your dreams, the egg timer you most lust after, and the pillowcases you simply must have. You will check these items on the list and turn them back in to the registry office. People who wish to buy you a gift go to the store, ask for the registry, and pick something out. Whatever they buy is taken off the list so that you don't wind up with fourteen bread makers.

Once upon a time, wedding registries were limited to large department stores and china shops. These days, they have become about as common as flies in a stable. This is a good thing. If you register at a place that only sells china, silverware, and crystal, there's a pretty good chance that you're only going to get china, silverware, and crystal. If you register at a place that sells a broader variety of wares, you greatly increase the odds of getting at least one present you like. After spending hours carefully analyzing the relative aesthetic and practical merits of "your" napkin rings, your fiancée might take pity and allow you to add something like a moderately cool corkscrew to the list.

There is, however, a loophole. Most wedding stuff comes in sets. Sets of china. Sets of silverware. Sets of crystal. Because these sets are so expensive, the pieces are bought individually. This creates a great opportunity. Let's say you only receive three of those expensive crystal goblets you had "your" heart set on. What are you going to do with three fancy glasses? You will either have to buy a bunch more, spending hundreds of dollars of your own cash, or bring those three back and make do with the perfectly nice glasses you got at Crate and Barrel. So you bring them back. At this point you may be able to convince your wife that you really need a new DVD player instead of yet another pair of candlesticks.

Can Anyone Say "Ka-Ching"?

All of this aside, you are almost certain to get one kind of gift that is both fun and practical: cash. Some people feel that cash is a cold and impersonal type of wedding gift. I heartily suggest you root these people out and avoid inviting them to your wedding. In fact, I encourage you to do everything possible to increase both the amount and percentage of cash gifts at your wedding. Just do this with all the tact and discretion you can muster.

First, it is considered outrageously garish to assume that anyone wants to buy you something for your wedding. Your invitations should not include where you are registered for gifts and should especially not include the fact that you really want unmarked c-notes. What you have to do is use the back channels to get the word out. Ask your parents, best man, and maid of honor to spread the word that you want money, lots of money, from the guests at your wedding. Encouraging cash gifts through these channels is marginally acceptable. Offering to accept Visa and MasterCard is not.

To make cash seem more gift-like, some couples have gone to the rather pathetic steps of "registering" at a local bank, realtor, or travel agent. While this does give people an idea of what you want to use the money for, it tends to complicate matters for no apparent purpose. Of course, this sort of sugarcoating is only necessary for those cultures that tend to find cash garish. If you are fortunate enough to descend from one of the great Asian or Mediterranean civilizations that showers the couple with crappy cards and nice checks, count your blessings. You will soon feel like a rich man, if only for one evening.

Thank You. Thank You. Thank You.

To repeat what your mom has told you a thousand times before, when someone sends you a present, you have to send him or her a thank-you note. Personally, I think this should be the same "you" who decided deep in your heart of hearts that the thing you most wanted from your rich Aunt Tilda was a set of porcelain salad tongs. Your fiancée may have other thoughts.

In any case, writing a thank-you note is no big deal. It's writing hundreds of them that hurts. For your average, run-of-the-list kind of presents, use this simple template:

> *Dear* [name or names] :
>
> *Thank you so much for the beautiful* [item]. *We will think of you whenever we* [see/use] *it.*
>
>
> *Fondly,*
>
> [Your names]

(Please note that the preceding template should not be used to express thanks for towels, sheets, or other items you use primarily when you are naked.)

For some special circumstances, the standard thank-you note just won't suffice. These tend to fall at both extremes. If someone has been so generous that you just have to do something bigger, invite him or her over for dinner or make a big show of it in some special way. The real fun, however, comes when someone sends you a gift that's so ugly and/or impractical it requires special commentary. For example:

Dear (name or names):

Thank you so much for the beautiful stuffed yak. This is one of the finest examples of the taxidermist's art currently in our possession. It will occupy a place of honor in our home, as soon as we have a home large enough to properly display such a treasure. (It really is quite a large yak, making your gift all the more generous.) Believe me, we will certainly think of you each and every time we pick our way around the yak in our home.

Fondly,

(Your names)

A Groom-Friendly Guide to Bridal Registeries

Store	Contact	Register for	Exchange it for
Target— Club Wedd	Any Target store or target.com	Oster 12-speed stand mixer	Game Boy Advance
Amazon	amazon.com	Le Creuset 11-inch nonstick sauté pan	Panasonic Progressive Scan DVD player
Sears	Any Sears store or sears.com	Cuisinart Plus food processor	Medalist table-tennis table
ACE Hardware	Participating stores	Hoover Wind-tunnel Upright	Black & Decker 10-inch power miter saw
Macy's	Any Macy's store or macys.com	Wedgewood Cornucopia tea-cup and saucer	Sharper Image wireless headphones

CHAPTER 19

The Prenuptial Celebrations

There are those who feel that a wedding is just too big an event to be celebrated with just one party. To prime the pump for the main event, these people hold a lengthy series of pre-wedding celebrations in the months leading up to the wedding. Among these are the engagement party, the bridal shower, the bachelor and bachelorette parties, and the rehearsal dinner.

Think of these as the social equivalent of stretching before you go into the game.

The Lightweight Stuff

What engagement parties and bridal showers lack in complexity, they can make up for in frequency. In some particularly party-mad homes, you might have several incarnations of both. This tends to happen most commonly when you and your fiancée hail from different ports or have divorced parents. Several sets of parents might want to throw their own engagement parties, and a couple of family friends might want to host showers. Keep in mind that engagement parties and bridal showers are often thrown as acts of revenge. After attending hundreds of these things for all their friends' kids, your mother, for example, may want to make sure she reaps the full harvest for your wedding.

This could be worse. Both engagement parties and bridal showers are mandatory present events. By multiplying the number of hits, you could substantially increase the number of gifts you will receive. You can expect a bunch of watered-down wedding gifts for engagement presents. The fun gifts, believe it or not, are actually more likely to come from your fiancée's shower. Yes, nine out of ten gifts will be some frilly, froufrou oddity that smells funny and looks like it was knitted by Mennonites. The other one out of ten will be lingerie, shockingly tantalizing lingerie in some cases. Now that's a gift any red-blooded American male can get behind.

The best part about both engagement parties and showers is that they are relatively low-impact events. Engagement parties are really just cocktail parties for family and friends. Yeah, you have to discuss your wedding plans with the tipsy old hens from your mom's bridge club, but it's easy to like people who just gave you a toaster oven. The bridal shower approaches perfection, largely because you don't even have to show up. Your fiancée has to spend an entire day eating cucumber sandwiches and cackling over wrapped boxes of hand towels, bathroom soap dispensers, and trampy white lingerie. At worst, you just show up at the end with a moving van, knock down a glass of champagne punch, and make off with the haul.

The Groom Shower

I went to one wedding a number of years back, where the groom insisted that it was unfair for the bride to have a shower when he didn't. He actually roped one of his dad's old friends into throwing him a tool shower. Stupid? Well, yeah. But he did walk away with an angle grinder, a chain saw, a nice socket set, and half a dozen cordless screwdrivers. Is this the kind of initiative that made this country great or what? Go ahead. See if you can find some sucker to throw you a shower, too. Just make sure that the invitees know what to bring as presents. The last thing you want to do is sit around with a bunch of guys opening boxes of potpourri and underwear.

The Bachelor Party

Enough of this lightweight claptrap. Let's get on with the sole-remaining male bastion in the entire wedding game: the bachelor party. By now you've heard some of the stories . . . mythic tales of weeklong benders with platoons of midget hookers, cattle troughs of Wild Turkey, and epic travels through seedy strip clubs in urban redevelopment zones. To hear the tales, you would think that the average bachelor party makes *Porky's* look like "Masterpiece Theatre."

Well, you've been to bachelor parties. How many of them looked like that to you? Yeah, I know, everyone did get pretty drunk. There were a lot of laughs and off-color jokes. You might have even left a few sawbucks in a G-string somewhere. But tell me true, Wild Man. Did you ever actually dance naked with a one-legged call girl in a tequila-filled hot tub? Did you even end the night with more tattoos than you began with? More likely, you rented a few skin flicks, played an unusually loud game of poker, and downed a six-pack of Old Milwaukee or something. That's OK. Just don't tell the girls that any bachelor party was that lame.

Technically speaking, the basic tone and tenor of your bachelor party is beyond your control. Your best man and/or other friends are perpetrating this on you, and you're just along for the ride. If you want to get a sense of how ugly this will get, just think about the other bachelor parties you've been to with this crowd. You should be in for similar treatment. If this is the first for your crew, watch out! A lot of guys will try to set the bar high on the first bachelor party. These things tend to get kind of old, and therefore tamer, as your posse ages.

While you may not be able to, or want to, control the full course of events at your bachelor party, I strongly suggest you follow a few basic rules. These could save you anywhere from one night to one lifetime's worth of grief:

- Never schedule your bachelor party for the night before your wedding unless you are certain only tea and crumpets will be served.
- If anything odd enters any of the stripper's orifices, make certain it isn't attached to you.
- There is nothing macho about drinking Long Island Ice Tea, Kamikazes, and Jell-O shots. If you want to be macho, drink moonshine with a sterno chaser.
- Friends don't let shit-faced friends drive anything but a Titleist.
- Your fiancée will desperately want to know what you did at your bachelor party. Don't tell her. If it was tame, she will lose respect for you. If it was wild, she will hurt you. Besides, all that curiosity is kind of cute.
- Remember, no matter how debauched your bachelor party might be, her bachelorette party is likely to be worse.

The Rehearsal Dinner

Sometimes referred to as "the last supper," your rehearsal dinner will be your last chance to break bread as a single man. This is a heck of a lot less significant than you might think. Consider your rehearsal to be sort of like the last scrimmage before the season starts. You'll go through all the same moves, but the intensity level is a whole lot lower.

The rehearsal dinner comes after (get this) the rehearsal. That is where everyone involved in the wedding comes together to learn their lines and walk through what they are supposed to do at the wedding. This is also an opportunity to realize how lame all of your closest friends and relatives really are. For example, your groomsmen might be told to walk down the aisle slowly, keeping pace with the bridesmaid with whom they have been paired. Then you witness Moe, Larry, Curly, and the rest of the gang galumphing down the aisle like they're looking for two empty seats in a packed movie house. Pathetic!

You should be aware of one rehearsal tradition, lest it catch you off guard. There is a remote possibility that your fiancée will be carrying a paper plate adorned with dozens of ribbons. Don't fret. She hasn't completely cracked under the pressure. This is simply a time-honored way for the bride to express her concerns that her future husband doesn't have the goods to please her in the marital bed. I wouldn't worry about it, Donkey Kong. Why would your fiancée need one of those?

Tradition dictates that the groom's parents host the post-rehearsal festivities. The idea behind this little soiree is to get the inner circle together for one last intimate evening before all hell breaks loose. Done right, this is a great chance for both sets of family and friends to get to know each other in a cordial, low-pressure setting. Done incorrectly, it can upstage the wedding, infuriate your in-laws, and douse the whole spirit of the weekend before it even gets started.

Here's how you head off the worst-case scenario. No matter how casual and simple your wedding, make sure your rehearsal dinner is far more casual and simple still. If your reception will be at all formal, this is pretty easy to pull off. If you are having a relatively simple wedding, on the other hand, you might just have to hold the rehearsal dinner at IHOP to make sure the competition doesn't get too stiff. This may create a problem with your mother. In some cases the mother of the groom will use the rehearsal dinner to prove to her friends and family that she can throw at least as good a party as her son's new in-laws. Discourage this as aggressively as possible. It will sow the seeds of discontent and make the whole thing a lot less fun than it should be.

As for the guest list, everyone at the rehearsal should be invited to the rehearsal dinner along with his or her spouse or date. Add any remaining parents, grandparents, godparents, and throw in all of your out-of-town guests. (This last bunch can be cut if you are getting married at some sort of resort where everyone will be an out-of-town guest.) Finally, you can round out the crew with a few special friends. This is a good idea if you had to diss a few people by not asking them to be in your wedding party.

Now all you have to do is sit back, chill out, and maybe make a nice toast at dinner. Tomorrow's the big day, Romeo, so resist the temptation to stay out all night with all of those friends you haven't seen for years. Maybe limit yourself to two body shots and a beer chaser, then off to bed with you.

CHAPTER 20

The Wedding Day

Welcome to the home stretch, Groom Boy. By nightfall, you'll have a big, dopey smile on your face and a bright, shiny chain on your ankle. You'll be tripping the light fantastic with a married woman and eating cake without a fork. This is going to be a great day.

So, how you feeling this morning? Got the sweaty mitts and cold dogs? Fret not, dear boy. It's only natural. You are, after all, about to commit yourself, body and soul, to one woman now and forever. In just a few short hours, you will stand before the assembled congregation and declare that you will never, ever, ever, ever have sex with anyone but your wife so long as you both shall live. That means never, not even when she gets all old and baggy and wears a colostomy bag under her size-56 muumuu. That means not if the Nymphomaniac Twins of Sweden Society invite you to be the keynote speaker at their next convention. Not ever, never, no sir. And, depending on the ceremony you're having, that's not just me talking. It's a mean and vengeful God.

Why would a guy get nervous about a silly thing like that?

Sure you might have a little bit of stage fright. They say that the average American is more afraid of public speaking than he is of dying. Well, today you may well be standing up in front of hundreds of people in an already emotionally charged situation. Don't worry. You probably won't forget your lines. Far more that half of all grooms don't split their pants when they kneel at the altar, and very few get pummeled with rotten fruit because their reception toasts were so hideously inappropriate and obtuse. I mean it's much more common for a groom to develop a hideous case of the flop sweats that soaks clear through his penguin suit and makes it difficult to keep his new ring on his finger. But don't worry; a little sweat never hurt anyone.

But seriously, let's say you do wake up that morning with doubts. What you basically have to do is just chill out. Yes, you are making a commitment; but no, you are not rushing into this. More important, you have somehow bamboozled some lovely thing into making the same commitment to you. If you are at all like every other man who ever walked the aisle, you are definitely getting the better half of that deal. Let's face it, you ain't no prize compared to the likes of her. When your hair has long stopped plugging the shower drain and you need a winch to haul your fat, lazy ass out of the La-Z-Boy, this relative hotty will still take pity on you at least three times a year (your birthday, your anniversary, and Valentine's Day). Count your blessings and hope that she doesn't read this chapter.

As for the stage fright, that one can be a bitch. Just remember that millions of guys do this every year, and only a few die from it. There's an old trick they teach aspiring meat puppets. When you start to feel stage fright, imagine your audience in their underwear.

This is supposed to humanize the crowd and lighten you up a bit. Depending on what some of your less-attractive guests might look like in their underwear, however, it might also induce vomiting. No one wants this. Probably the best thing to do is just keep breathing deeply, buck up, and get on with it. It's kind of like that time you lost your virginity in the back of mom's Caravan. You can be really nervous and have fun at the same time.

I will offer this: the most important thing to do when you wake up this morning is something. Anything. Just don't sit around working yourself up into a tizzy. Go for a long walk, get some of the guys together for a softball game, play a round of golf, anything. Just make sure it's something that can't possibly go wrong and make you late for the ceremony. In other words, no "Jackass" stunts, no skydiving, and no long trips that could get you stuck in traffic.

As I mentioned earlier, it's also a great idea to schedule your photo session for before the wedding ceremony. It digs heavily into the freak-out hours and gives everyone a little bit of buffer time before the ceremony. It's not good to be late for the pictures. It's really bad to be late for your wedding. That, my friend, is strictly the bride's prerogative.

The Wedding Itself

At this point, there is little I can tell you that will help you make it through your wedding ceremony. Just relax and do what the officiant says. Unless, of course, your fiancée says to do something else. I would walk you through the steps, but there are just too many variations on the theme to cover here. It would be too easy to get mixed up and cause social tension and perhaps even mass hysteria. For example, at a Jewish wedding you wrap a glass in a napkin and stomp on it. Try this at a Catholic wedding and you will be arrested for vandalism.

However, just to give you a little context, here are some of the more charming wedding customs you will likely eschew. When your rituals start seeming really odd (and let's face it, they are all really odd), be thankful you don't have to do any of this:

- Some remote tribal wedding guides might begin, "After completing your ritual circumcision . . ."
- At one point it was an accepted practice to hang bloody sheets out of the honeymooning couple's window to prove to the village that the bride had been a virgin.
- Various cultures would see you tarted up with everything from a thick glazing of cocoa butter to a fresh set of self-induced scars before strutting you down the aisle.

Now let's hear you whine about having to sit through a full mass just to get hitched.

At the Reception

Your wedding reception officially begins as soon as you and your wife clear the aisle. This can be one of those truly great moments in your life. After all the planning, emotion, arguing, and expense, you two lovebirds are now an old married couple. Better yet, your wedding is now just a big, fat party. You will have a chance to revel in this for anywhere from thirty seconds to two minutes. Then it's time to get in place for . . . the receiving line. (You know those blood-curdling screams they do in horror flicks? Insert one of those here.)

A quaint tradition modeled on the license-plate renewal procedures at the DMV, the receiving line consists of making everyone you know wait on a single line for up to one hour. This is done for the sole purpose of offering congratulations to you and the missus. As if that weren't bad enough, they must also offer congratulations to your bride's mom and dad, your mom and dad, and sometimes all of the grandparents, your best man, the maid of honor, bridesmaids, and groomsmen.

If everyone would just line up like they do at the end of a hockey game and quickly breeze down the line, the receiving line would be no big deal. Unfortunately this has never, ever happened. Almost always, at least one wayward aunt, oblivious to the 185 people in line behind her, will strike up a conversation about her own wedding, your future plans, the price of tea in China, or whatever else strikes her fancy. If anyone on the receiving line has even the least bit of reluctance to shut this woman up, the process will come to a slow, grinding, eight-car-pileup halt. The only way to deal with this sort of cretin is to interrupt her mid-sentence and say one of two things:

1. "Shut your pie hole, you old windbag. Can't you see you're holding up the line?"
2. "Thanks so much for being here. We'll see you at the reception."

Then quickly turn to the next person in line and greet him or her. The only other solution to this problem is to cut out the receiving line altogether. Let's call that one "the preferred option."

The Toasts

At some point during your reception, there will be a series of toasts to you, your bride, and your parents. The best man traditionally kicks things off by toasting the bride. The father of the bride then rises to toast the happy couple. You're up next, then your wife, then all hell breaks loose.

Let me give you a little tip here. You don't want to start thinking about your toast as you rise to deliver it. This will get you in serious trouble. You don't need to write the whole thing out, but you really should have a pretty clear idea of what you want to say. Here's what those ideas should be. You love your wife. You thank her parents. You thank your parents. You appreciate everyone coming here to share this day with you. Now it's up to you to make those thoughts sweet and charming and maybe a little funny. And believe me, when I say a little funny I mean a little funny. Go for the big yucks and you will sound like some pathetic hack comic working the smaller rooms in the Catskills.

"Today, I officially became the luckiest man on earth," is a good opener for your toast. "Take my wife, please," is not.

Trip the Light Fantastic

You've seen this one in the movies. The lights dim, the crowd gathers round, the handsome groom and beautiful bride take the dance floor. And as they elegantly float around the room we fade to black. Roll credits. Your first dance should feel like that, except that the groom will be uglier and the bride will not be some anorexic semi-starlet working her way up from hand lotion commercials.

The key here is to make sure that "your song" is playing for your first dance. If you don't have a "your song," you best hurry up and get one. And while you're at it, sign up for some dancing lessons. You look like a booze-addled musk ox out there.

Your first dance of the evening has to be with your wife. After that, your dance card should include your mom, the bride's mom, the maid of honor, your grandmothers, and stepmothers. After that, you're on your own.

Cutting the Cake

Cutting the cake is a sparkly highlight of the wedding reception. Done well, it makes for a nice series of photo ops. You have the handsome couple in front of the frilly cake shot. There's the happy-couple-holding-the-knife shot. The bride-daintily-feeding-the-groom-cake shot. The groom-smushing-a-great-gob-of-cake-into-the-bride's-mug shot. The chocolate-frosting-cascading-down-the-bride's-pristine-white-gown shot. The bride-kneeing-the-groom-in-the-gonads shot. The groom-doubled-over-in-agony shot. It really creates a very dramatic little sequence in the old wedding album. Even better, you could make a little flip book and run it to that "The Bride Cuts the Cake" song.

Throwing Stuff

Some believe that the bridal-bouquet toss is an outmoded custom. Sure, it clearly implies that what every single woman in the room wants most is to be a married woman. Sure, it turns any real yearnings to be wed into a desperate display of thinly veiled female aggression. There is always that awkward moment when the women who really want to catch the thing try to do so without looking like they are trying too hard. I hate that. Yes, sir, something's not right. I propose that all future bouquet tosses be handled thusly. Before the toss, all single women would strip down to bikinis and enter a large pool filled with Jell-O. You take it from there.

From my perch, the garter toss thing is even weirder. First, you start with this little, "I see London, I see France" thing as you slowly give your great-uncle Chuck a chance to get a gander at your new wife's skivvies. Then you wing this outmoded bit of hosiery at your single guy friends, all of whom are required to make a great show of ducking it. If you have any arm at all, the garter will land on some poor sucker, who must place it on the leg of the alpha female who muscled her way in to catch the bouquet. Much of this will be done to musical accompaniment.

You may be shocked to hear that this little pair of routines is still performed at a substantial portion of weddings in this country. (And we make fun of people who only exchange a few goats at their wedding receptions. Talk about living in glass houses.) I think you should perform them at yours, unless, of course, you would prefer a simple exchange of angoras.

Working the Room

You'll hear more than a few people tell you that the bride and groom never get to eat their meals at the reception. This is probably because you'll spend the better part of the meal walking from table to table greeting your guests. This will be kind of fun, especially for the first few tables. You two will flit in like Scott and Zelda, all swank-a-riffic-like. You'll spark a bit of gaiety, throw in a few bon mots, and breeze off to the next table. If you have the right kind of guests, you may even leave that first table with three or four envelopes full of cash.

I'm guessing that you'll be able to keep the mood going for the first half a dozen tables or so. After that, you start to realize that you've said all of this before. You've answered these questions already, and your face is starting to hurt from smiling. You feel a lot less like Scott and Zelda.

Ten tables in and you are starting to feel the burn. Your feet hurt. You're getting tired. You look over to see that your dinner has been cleared, even though you didn't get a bite of it. By the last table, you can barely stand. You want to skip it, but you know you can't. Stoically, you discuss your honeymoon plans for the fourteenth time. And yes, it was a lovely ceremony, wasn't it? You resist the temptation to just demand the checks and go sit down.

As a form of revenge for putting you through the table-visit paddle wheel, you get to play with the seating chart. This can really be good fun. First, you get to pick really fun people for the bridal party who sit at your table. Then you get to punish people you don't like much by sticking them with other obnoxious people. Does your wife have an annoying cousin who can't stop whining? Stick her in between a bald septuagenarian with bad body odor and the six-year-old who hasn't quite mastered that chewing-with-your-mouth-closed thing.

With all of that, Mr. Married Man, your wedding is complete. Now you go and have yourself a good time consummating this thing.

CHAPTER 21

The Honeymoon

The first thing you'll want to know about your honeymoon is that you really want a good one. You want to take a trip that's cooler, more expensive, and more exotic than any trip you've ever taken. And you want to do it very shortly after your wedding. You want this for three reasons. First, because you can. Second, because you will really need a long break to unwind from the wedding stress. And third, because honeymoon nookie is flat-out better than almost any other flavor of nookie there is. This is not an opportunity to be lightly missed.

Tradition has it that the planning of the honeymoon is the only part of the wedding festivities that is fully the groom's responsibility. That means that, traditionally, honeymoons were the most ill-considered and shabbily planned part of the entire process. (You think everyone in the continental United States used to honeymoon in Niagara Falls because they liked falling water so much?) Fortunately, more and more brides have become more and more involved in the honeymoon planning process. This generally fortunate development has been a bit of a double-edged sword. On the downside, you are now far less likely to spend your honeymoon marlin fishing. On the upside, your "honeymoon suite" is now much more likely to come with an indoor flush toilet. Let's call that one a draw.

For our purposes, let's say that the initial planning of the honeymoon will be your responsibility. Stepping in to change all of your decisions and correct all of your boneheaded mistakes will fall to her.

Which Way Do We Go? Which Way Do We Go?

When it comes to planning your honeymoon, you certainly have plenty of options. With a once-in-a-lifetime travel budget, you could easily afford to go see, up close and in person, one of the true wonders of the world. You could watch the sun set over the Taj Mahal as the strains of the sitar waft through the gentle Indian evening. You could witness the majestic migration of the wildebeest across the Serengeti Plain. You could join the annual running of the morons at Pamplona. You could do almost anything, anywhere.

So what are you going to do? You're going to plunk your fat, lazy butt in a midgrade resort beach chair and swill fruity tropical drinks from plastic tiki cups, aren't you? Sure you'll grab your little taste of adventure. Between rounds one afternoon you'll take the helicopter ride over the local volcano. That should help you work up a thirst.

It might not surprise you to discover that the vast majority of American honeymooners head straight to one of the world's great beach-potato meccas. These hot spots include Hawaii, the Caribbean, Bermuda, and the Mexican coasts. If you wish to travel even farther, you might also consider Tahiti, Bali, or the Seychelles.

The difference between these tropical paradises can be striking. For example, in Hawaii you might check in to a large, all-inclusive resort beautifully landscaped with palm trees and exotic tropical flowers. Water will flow everywhere. You'll flop on the pristine beach looking out over the turquoise water, then maybe play a round of golf. Perhaps you'll cap off the evening at an "authentic" luau with fire jugglers, roast pig, and poi. On the other hand, let's say you go to the Caribbean. You might check in to a large, all-inclusive resort beautifully landscaped with palm trees and exotic tropical flowers. Water will flow everywhere. You'll flop on the pristine beach looking out over the turquoise water, then maybe play a round of golf. Maybe you'll cap off the evening at an "authentic" Caribbean beach party with fire jugglers, roast goat, and conch fritters.

In other words, you don't want to make any rash decisions. Before you decide on which tropical island will be best for your honeymoon, make sure you and your wife agree on which kind of animal you want to see roasted on a spit. Just in case, you might also want to choose a location that has a few points of interest other than the swim-up bars. After a week or so, even the prettiest beaches can get kind of old. It's nice to have the option to go off and see some interesting ruins or something for half a day. If nothing else, it will make your mai tais seem better deserved that evening.

Honeymoons for City Slickers

Some people have decided that they want more from their honeymoons than a blistering sunburn and an unusual item of native headgear. These intrepid newlyweds will head off to the great cultural capitals of Europe, purportedly to contrast and compare the collections of Romanesque statuary at the Uffizi, Louvre, and Prado. (Note to art lovers: if there is no such thing as Romanesque statuary, please accept my apologies. Then shut up.) These motives are invariably a lie. The only real reason to honeymoon in Europe is to have sex in as many countries as possible, as soon as possible. So skip the pretense, buy a Eurailpass with sleeper car privileges and log yourself as many of those candy-ass little European nations as your libido can handle.

Actually, a European honeymoon can be a great way to get your wedding off to a good start while helping to tighten the bonds of friendship between nations. Here are a few tips:

- All French people should be expected to speak English. In fact, if we didn't save their lame asses in World War II, there would still be beer halls lining the Champs-Elysées. A polite reminder of this historical fact is well appreciated by most Parisians.
- "German" is an English word. In Europe, Germans refer to themselves as "The Hun."
- Contrary to popular opinion, the food in London is excellent. For a real treat, try the sheep-brain pudding with a nice tall glass of warm beer.
- Go into a "coffeehouse" in Amsterdam and ask for coffee. It's always good for a laugh.

Of course, you need not go to Europe to be dissed by snotty maître d's and robbed by foul-smelling street thugs. Many American cities offer these same pleasures. When it comes to effete waiters with bad attitudes, New York can compete with any city in creation. And why go all the way to Paris to find people who don't bathe when San Francisco is just a short domestic flight away? Chicago, bitchin' city that it is, should never be a honeymoon destination for the same reason that flannel pajamas should never be the honeymoon sleepwear.

The Love Boat

It's easy to understand why a growing number of couples choose an ocean voyage for their honeymoon. In fact, it's all laid out for you right in the brochure. Donning formal attire, you will dine in the company of dukes and duchesses and at the captain's table. You'll enjoy romantic walks on the empty, moonlit decks. There will be making out in vintage coaches in the hold. Maybe you'll even get the chance to witness one of those colorful gypsy dance parties among the peasants in steerage.

The reality may differ slightly. Instead of the dukes and duchesses at the captain's table, you are more likely to find about eighty-tons of American tourists obliterating the buffet like a Mack truck hitting a watermelon cart. Those moonlit walks are likely to be in the company of four-dozen pensioners blowing chunks over the rail. And the last time I checked, the only things in the hold were slot machines, and the only people in steerage were more fat Hoosiers with AARP cards. Of course, that doesn't mean that you can't have a great honeymoon on a cruise. You just have to be pretty sure you are picking the right one. This is one area where you want to talk to a travel agent about which cruises draw which crowds. This will make as great an impact on your vacation as the destinations you are visiting. Remember, once the boat pulls up the gangplanks, you are stuck with the people on board until the next stop.

Speaking of stops, most cruises these days make a bunch of them. Where you want your boat to stop, of course, should be one of the prime factors you take into consideration when booking a cruise. If you book a Bermudan cruise, for example, the eighty-seven T-shirt shops along Front Street will sell shirts with sayings like, "Hamilton, Bermuda. A quaint drinking village with a fishing problem." On the other hand, if you book an Alaska cruise, the seventy-four T-shirt shops on Front Street will sell shirts saying things like, "Juneau, Alaska. A quaint drinking village with a fishing problem."

Decisions. Decisions. Decisions.

Disney and Vegas

I'm going to take a flyer here. If you are not going to the beach, the boat, or Europe, I'm guessing that you are one of the increasingly barbaric horde who has decided to kick off their wedded life in either Disney World or Las Vegas. I lump these unbearably disturbing destinations together because they are so difficult to distinguish. One has throngs of costumed performers, pirate rides, and elaborate roller coasters. The other is Disney World.

Both the Magic Kingdom and the Sinful City offer special opportunities to the honeymooning couple. Disney lets you spend your first day as husband and wife waiting in line to shake hands with someone in a Mickey Mouse costume. Las Vegas gives you a great opportunity to get rid of all of that pesky wedding-present cash in one evening at the craps table. The combination offers something truly special. It allows you to decide which side of puberty you would like your adolescent behavior to fall on.

Book It, Dano

Once you and the squeeze decide on a honeymoon destination, it's time to get busy with the details. If you're smart, you'll go to a decent travel agent, look through the brochures, and make the call. All you have to do then is tell him or her when you want to go and how much you want to spend. The agent will take care of everything from there. Of course, it never hurts to check a place out in as many ways as possible before you plunk down your cash. Ask around and see if you can find anyone who's been there. If that doesn't net anything, at least look at the website and give them a call to see if you can trip them up. Find out if any construction is planned for the time you expect to be staying there. Make sure you understand what all the charges will be including taxes and service fees. In some extreme cases this can add more than 20 percent to your bill.

With all the Internet sources now available, you may find that you can get a better deal on your own rather than through a travel agent. This will take a little more legwork than going the agent route, but it might just be worth it. Browse around Expedia.com, Travelocity.com, CheapTickets.com, and priceline.com and see if you find anything interesting. They all cover airfare, hotels, and rental cars. Several also have some good deals on all-inclusive packages. Even if you decide you want a travel agent to handle all the arrangements for you, it wouldn't hurt to look around these websites first to give you a general sense of what your options are and how much they cost. Having some background knowledge may just take a little of that babe-in-the-woods shine off of you.

If you really want to go off the beaten track, you may have to do your homework the old-fashioned way. Go to a library or bookstore, get a stack of travel guides, and start working the phones. You'll find a certain charm in doing things this way, but it's rarely necessary. There's little in a travel book that you won't find online. When you do find it online, the information will be more current and you'll be able to make reservations right away.

This shouldn't have to be said, but let's face it. Guys like us generally have to ask someone else where we left our shoes. When you shell out major simoleons for something like a honeymoon, look before you leap. If something sounds too cheap to be true, be careful. It probably is.

Timing Your Exit

For flat-out panache, it's hard to beat the happy couple driving away from the reception, tin cans clanging, heading straight off on a dream honeymoon. Yeah, it makes for a cool exit, but there are some fundamental problems with the approach. First, your reception is going to be packed with people you like to party with, including some who you haven't seen in a while. You may not want to close the party down, but you probably won't want to skip out early, either. Far more important, when you do want to skip out, it won't be because you're all itchy to get on an airplane. If it is, you just married the wrong girl, friend.

Far more likely, you'll want to spend your wedding night within a couple of miles from your reception. If your friends are anything like mine, I would caution you to not let anyone know where you are going. Even better, tell all of them that you are flying out that night. All those pranks they think will be really funny, won't be.

In any case, book your flight out for sometime the day after your wedding, preferably in the late afternoon. It's always tempting to get an early flight to stretch the time you get to spend on vacation. This is one time when it won't be worth it. Give yourself the morning to sleep in, have breakfast sent up, and take a leisurely trip out to the airport. This will make for a better start than a bleary-eyed panic run at 5 A.M. after only three hours of sleep.

Happily
Ever After

etting married is not quite the life-transforming event it
was back in the days of premarital virginity and big fins
on Cadillacs. I'll go out on a limb here and guess that your wedding night will not be the first time you discover which side of the
bed your wife likes to sleep on. In fact, if you didn't already split
the rent bill before the wedding, you probably had yourself more
than a few slumber parties.

So what's the big deal? Being married does have legal consequences, but we already covered that part. And who really cares

about that, anyway? What we're talking about here is what it all feels like at the end of the wedding day.

So does being married feel different than being not married? Yes. No. Maybe. I don't know.

Being married feels like you are part of a bigger family and a grander tradition. Saying "my wife" feels really different from saying "my girlfriend." And it's fun tapping your wedding ring on the steering wheel when a good tune comes on the radio. The rest you'll just have to find out for yourself.

I will offer you one last word of unwanted advice. Don't try to make being married change you more than it wants to. You didn't become more responsible when you said, "I do." You just sounded that way to other people. If you think that an hour in church and a piece of cake will somehow magically transform you into Ward Cleaver, you are not a married man. You are an idiot. The same goes double for your expectations of your wife. If her greatest pleasure was dancing on cowboy bars, it's really unlikely that she'll suddenly want to stay at home knitting just because she wore a big white dress one evening.

Both of you still are who you are. You've just promised to be that together. And that's just about the best thing there is.

With that, you are on your own, my married friend. Welcome to the club.

Helpful Lists

TEN THINGS YOU NEED TO KNOW TO GET HAPPILY MARRIED

1. Propose to someone with a good sense of humor. She'll need it.
2. It doesn't matter how much you spend on an engagement ring, as long as it is more than you can afford.
3. She will not promise to "obey" you. Don't ask.
4. Have at least one good argument about a detail of your wedding plans, just to show you care.
5. When you lose this argument, lose graciously.
6. Carry a handkerchief during the ceremony. She's going to need one and wedding gowns don't have pockets.
7. In your wedding toast, make sure to thank your wife, your parents, and her parents.
8. Have at least one glass of water between every drink at your reception, and don't forget to eat something.
9. Don't forget to pack birth control for your wedding night.
10. Nothing will be perfect. Not your ceremony, not your reception, not your wife, not your children, and certainly not you. Expect perfection and you guarantee disappointment. Embrace imperfection, and you open yourself to all manner of happy surprises.

TEN THINGS YOU NEED TO KNOW TO STAY HAPPILY MARRIED

1. The secret to a happy marriage is a selective lack of communication.
2. Having two bathrooms doesn't hurt either.
3. Nothing can be gained by comparing your wife to your mother. Ever.
4. The same goes for comparing her to her mother . . . times infinity.
5. Don't cheat on her.
6. Lie all the time, but don't lie maliciously.
7. Never forget her birthday or your anniversary.
8. Buying her something expensive doesn't automatically get you out of the doghouse, but it doesn't hurt.
9. When you fight about money, remember that divorces are far more expensive than whatever it is you are fighting about.
10. Never stop dating her. Never let her forget why you started.

FIVE SYNONYMS FOR *WIFE* THAT WILL NOT AMUSE THE OLD BALL AND CHAIN

1. The old ball and chain
2. The old lady
3. The old battle ax
4. Anything else with *the old* in it
5. The purchasing department

THE TEN BEST THINGS ANYONE HAS EVER SAID ABOUT MARRIAGE

"I married beneath me. All women do."

—Lady Nancy Astor

"I think men who have a pierced ear are better prepared for marriage. They've experienced pain and bought jewelry."

—Rita Rudner

"My mother said it was simple to keep a husband: you must be a maid in the living room, a cook in the kitchen, and a whore in the bedroom. I said, 'hire the other two and I'll take care of the bedroom.'"

—Jerry Hall

"My own or other people's?"

—Peggy Guggenheim, in response to the question,
"How many husbands have you had?"

"Behind every successful man is a surprised mother-in-law."

—Anonymous

"Many a man owes his success to his first wife and his second wife to his success."

—Jim Backus

"Never tell. Not if you love your wife. . . . In fact, if your old lady walks in on you, deny it. Yeah. Just flat out and she'll believe it: 'I'm tellin' ya. This chick came downstairs with a sign around her neck "Lay on Top of Me or I'll Die." I didn't know what I was gonna do.'"

—Lenny Bruce

"The only thing that holds a marriage together is the husband bein' big enough to keep his mouth shut, to step back, and see where his wife is wrong."

—Archie Bunker

"The most happy marriage I can imagine to myself would be the union of a deaf man to a blind woman."

—Samuel Coleridge

171

"Love is an ideal thing, marriage a real thing; a confusion of the real with the ideal never goes unpunished."

—Goethe

A SAMPLER OF VEGAS WEDDING CHAPELS

Tired of the expensive hassles of planning a traditional wedding? Get yourself a white Cadillac convertible, and head to Las Vegas, home of the $29 drive-thru wedding:

Viva Las Vegas Wedding Chapel
1205 Las Vegas Boulevard South
Las Vegas, NV 89104
702-384-0771

> *The popular Elvis Blue Hawaii Wedding Package features an Elvis impersonator to perform the ceremony at a shrine dedicated to the King. The package includes a choice between two hula dancers or a Priscilla impersonator, theatrical lighting and fog, and two songs by "Elvis," all for a lousy $700. If you want to add Marilyn, Cher, or Donna Summers, it'll cost an extra $250 a pop. Other themes are available.*

Graceland Wedding Chapel
619 Las Vegas Boulevard South
Las Vegas, NV 89101
702-382-0091

> *Basic ceremony $65. The King's package with the ceremony performed by Elvis, flowers, wedding video, pictures, limo service, garter, floral spray for bride, souvenir T-shirts, and so forth is $495.*

Las Vegas Wedding Chapels
231 Las Vegas Boulevard South
Las Vegas, NV 89101
702-382-9830

*Drive-through, limousine, strip chapels, western-theme
weddings, rooftop weddings, or your dream wedding in a
chapel fit for a princess. Drive-through weddings on the strip
start at $29.*

LasVegasWeddings.com
2770 S. Maryland Parkway Suite 506
Las Vegas, NV 89109
888-30-MARRY

*A wide assortment of theme weddings ranging from your
traditional Elvis and fairy-tale weddings to Gothic,
intergalactic, Egyptian, gangster, and "Viva Las Vegas." Most
run $500–$600. Packages for a quick chapel ceremony and
a room at a casino start at about $400.*

Star Trek Wedding
7231 Eastern Avenue, Suite 102
Las Vegas, NV 89119
877-914-4490

*Get married on the bridge of the USS Enterprise 1701-D by
a Star Fleet officer. Package includes photos, bride's
bouquet, groom's boutonniere, limo service, witness, and
tips. All for $749 U.S. (Federation currency not accepted.)*